Shadow Courts
The Tribunals That
Rule Global Trade

COLUMBIA GLOBAL REPORTS
NEW YORK

Shadow Courts
The Tribunals That Rule Global Trade

Haley Sweetland Edwards

Shadow Courts:
The Tribunals That Rule Global Trade
Copyright © 2016 by Haley Sweetland
Edwards

Published by Columbia Global Reports
91 Claremont Avenue, Suite 515
New York, NY 10027
globalreports.columbia.edu
facebook.com/columbiaglobalreports
@columbiaGR

Library of Congress Control Number:
2016945881
ISBN: 978-0-9971264-0-2

Book design by Strick & Williams
Map design by Jeffrey L. Ward
Author photograph by Keith Mellnick

Printed in the United States of America

Shadow Courts
The Tribunals That Rule Global Trade

CONTENTS

Acknowledgments

A huge thank you to the dozens of lawyers, negotiators, arbitrators, activists, and policymakers who, over the course of my reporting this book, gave me hours of their personal time in interviews. I am particularly grateful to those who disagreed with me and yet, quite out of step with modern times, engaged with me anyway, talking through each point with patience and grace. This book is better for it. An extra thanks to those practicing lawyers who, had they billed the hours they spent talking with me, would be today many thousands of dollars richer.

I am also deeply indebted to the goodhearted people—Todd Tucker, Rachel Wellhausen, Henry Farrell, Jay Newton-Small, and Barry Lynn—who read versions along the way. Thank you for your shrewd insight, criticism, and support. The inadequacies of the book are mine; the good bits are thanks to you. Many thanks also to my editors Nicholas Lemann and Jimmy

So, publisher Camille McDuffie, and to friends and colleagues at   11
Time magazine for letting me shirk my duties for a bit to write
on international investment law.

And last but certainly not least, thank you to my husband,
Paul Stephens, my parents, Jane Sweetland and Lee Edwards,
and all my wonderful family, genetic and otherwise, including
The Compound of greater northeast D.C., for your enduring
support. I am so grateful to all of you.

Introduction

The environmental activist Jane Kleeb was driving down Highway 281 near Lincoln, Nebraska, on a gray day in January 2016, when she got a call from a reporter.

At the time, Kleeb was still riding high off of her success organizing local farmers, ranchers, and environmentalists in opposition to the Keystone XL pipeline, which would have carried petroleum products from Canada's tar sands across the Nebraska plains to the Gulf of Mexico. Thanks to her and other activists' efforts, President Barack Obama had announced in November 2015 that his administration would deny the Canadian company TransCanada permission to move forward with the project, ending an eight-year-long effort to get the pipeline built.

The reporter was calling to ask Kleeb about a new twist in the saga. Earlier that day, TransCanada had announced it was suing the U.S. government for $15 billion on the grounds that Obama's decision to block the project violated the North American Free Trade Agreement. It was the first Kleeb had heard of the suit. "I'm an organizer, so my reaction was, 'When are the hearings? Where is this happening? Who's the judge?'" she said recently. If TransCanada was challenging the decision in court, she wanted to be there. Could she protest on the court-house steps? Arrange for a rally in a nearby town?

But that, Kleeb learned, was not how this case would go down. TransCanada wasn't suing the U.S. in a U.S. court, or in a Canadian court for that matter. Its argument would not be heard by a judge, and the merits of the case would not be considered under the auspices of either country's legal system. There would be no protest on any courthouse steps. Instead, the case would be heard by a tribunal, manned by three private arbitrators, operating under a supranational legal system that Kleeb had never heard of. "It was totally strange," she told me. "A foreign company can sue us in some secret tribunal? How is that even possible?"

Investor-state dispute settlement, or ISDS, first appeared in treaties in 1969. The idea behind the mechanism was straightforward: If a foreign investor believed that his host country—the nation where his company was operating—had violated an international treaty by seizing or destroying his factories, oil fields, or other assets, he could file an ISDS claim directly against that country. He could do that without involving his own government and without having to wait endlessly for a developing country's corrupt or biased court system to dispense judgment.

By filing an ISDS claim, the investor would trigger the formation of a special arbitration tribunal, which would exist temporarily outside the jurisdiction of any nation's judiciary or any international body. Its sole purpose would be to determine how much, if anything, the country owed the investor in compensation for property that had been seized or demolished. For example, in the late 1980s, the Sri Lankan government destroyed a British seafood company's shrimp-processing plant during a military raid on rebels. The British investor filed an ISDS claim, a tribunal was formed, and the arbitrators determined that the Sri Lankan government must pay the company $460,000 in compensation for the destroyed plant. That was it. Case closed. The British company did not have to rely on Sri Lankan courts. The episode did not become a major diplomatic incident. The U.K. did not have to step in to defend its investors' interests.

And that was the whole point: ISDS was supposed to be a cool, efficient, and apolitical dispute resolution system that kept powerful nations from interfering in the affairs of weaker countries, and that offered an extra layer of protection for foreign investors operating in countries with unreliable courts. But in the last 20 years, the mechanism has quietly changed, evolving into something much more powerful—and very political indeed.

One factor in this evolution is the explosion of new claims. Between the 1960s and 2000, ISDS was almost never used. Investors brought about 40 claims total in 40 years. Since 2000, there have been 647. In 2015 alone, there were 70 new cases. That uptick is partly because there are thousands more treaties today that include ISDS. For the last 25 years, countries have signed

thousands of bilateral investment treaties, and beginning in
the 1990s, nearly every new trade agreement, from NAFTA and
Central American Free Trade Agreement to the Energy Charter,
included a chapter on investment, complete with ISDS. In 1989,
there were just a few hundred agreements that included ISDS.
As of 2015, there were more than 3,000.

Another reason for the explosion of new claims is that
the definition of what it means for a sovereign nation to seize
or destroy a foreign company's property, or otherwise violate
an investor's property rights under the terms of an investment treaty, has become much more expansive. Investors now
regularly file claims if their host government passes a new
law or regulation that results in even a partial loss of a company's property or impinges in some way on its future profits.
For example, in TransCanada's ISDS claim against the U.S., it
argues that President Obama's decision to cancel the Keystone
XL pipeline violated NAFTA by expropriating the company's
expected *future* profits.

That modern interpretation has only cropped up in the
last 20 years, but it has opened up a vast new gray area. Where
ISDS claims were once about seized oil fields and bulldozed
factories, now they are about tax increases and environmental
regulations. Where is the line between a government's right to
regulate in the public interest and a foreign corporation's claim
to its own property?

Meanwhile, the directionality of ISDS claims has also
changed. In the 1960s and '70s, the idea was that investors
would use ISDS as a means to get compensation from a developing country with corrupt or rickety rule of law, where there

16 were no other avenues of receiving justice. But nowadays, investors regularly use it to challenge well-developed countries with
robust court systems, including the U.S., Canada, Australia, and
Germany, where there are very clearly other avenues of receiving justice. That reality has made this supposedly apolitical tool
of dispute resolution a hot button issue. Why should some rich
Canadian investor get to do an end-run around the U.S. court
system? Why should powerful, multinational corporations get
access to a special, supranational judicial system that no one
else can use? Why is there no way to appeal an ISDS award?

U.S. trade negotiators are now working to include ISDS in as
many new treaties as possible, including both of the massive
new free trade deals coming down the pike. The Trans-Pacific
Partnership, which President Obama signed in February 2016
and which Congress will likely ratify before he leaves office,
already includes ISDS. Whether the mechanism will be inserted
into the Transatlantic Trade and Investment Partnership, linking the U.S. and Europe, is a subject of controversy. The question
has already catalyzed something of an intellectual civil war in
Europe, with the European Parliament recently rejecting, across
party lines, any treaty that includes ISDS. Protesters opposed
to it have swamped the streets in Berlin, Paris, and Brussels and
written hundreds of letters in opposition to what they see as
the imposition of shadowy "corporate courts" that can be used
to undermine laws and regulations and compromise national
sovereignty.

U.S. trade negotiators say such rhetoric is overblown. They
point out that the U.S. is already a signatory to 50 agreements

that include ISDS, and that foreign corporations have only ever
used it to challenge Washington 18 times. The U.S. hasn't yet
lost a case. But experts on both sides of the debate argue those
stats undersell the importance of ISDS. Including the mechanism in the TPP and TTIP would forever alter the global legal
landscape for investors. The U.S.'s 50 existing treaties are relatively tiny, representing just 10 percent of the U.S.'s foreign
direct investment; including ISDS in the TPP would increase
that ratio significantly. If ISDS is included in both those trade
deals, it would mean that any corporation headquartered in
any of the nations that are signatories to either treaty—that
includes the vast majority of companies listed under the Global
Fortune 500—could use the mechanism to challenge U.S. laws
and regulations outside of U.S. courts, in the same way that
TransCanada is today.

"I don't think the question is whether U.S. laws will get challenged by foreign corporations under the TPP," Simon Lester, a
trade expert at the libertarian Cato Institute, told me recently.
"It's pretty clear the U.S. will be challenged and it will lose some
of those challenges and the U.S. taxpayers will have to pay."

ISDS has yet to become a big news item in the U.S. Aside from a
few op-eds and a proliferation of mostly error-riddled "explain-
ers" on the subject, it has remained largely the purview of trade
wonks. One reason is that ISDS does not follow the normal contours of the free trade debate. You can be 100 percent in favor of
free trade and still be against ISDS.

Take libertarians, for example. They are the staunchest
intellectual defenders of free trade deals, and yet have been

18 among the loudest critics of ISDS, which they see not as a liberalizing tool, but as the opposite: ISDS gives certain economic players an advantage over everyone else. Only foreign investors can use the mechanism; domestic investors can't. In a globalized economy, how does that make sense? Why should Toyota, which is technically a foreign company, despite its vast manufacturing operation in the U.S., be afforded a special judicial privilege that allows it to challenge U.S. laws outside of U.S. courts, when GM and Ford do not have access to that same perk?

Libertarians also point out that ISDS allows foreign corporations to target laws and regulations that threaten their economic dominance. Just recently, for example, the U.S. pharmaceutical giant Eli Lilly filed an ISDS claim against Canada after the country passed a law limiting the lifespan of drug patents. The law was designed to create a freer market—to reduce pharmaceutical companies' monopoly control and to allow more generic competition in the drug industry—but Eli Lilly says it violates NAFTA by expropriating its future profits.

Many dyed-in-the-wool conservatives, a group that has also traditionally backed free trade, object to ISDS too, but for different reasons. Joined by a growing number of state and local legislators, they worry that the mechanism will be used to undermine state and local laws. The National Conference of State Legislatures has promised it will not support any trade deal that includes ISDS. Conservatives also see ISDS as an unbearable imposition on American sovereignty, and reject it on the same grounds that they have long refused to confirm the U.S. as a member of the International Criminal Court or other binding international treaties, like the Convention on the Elimination of All Forms of Discrimination Against Women.

Constitutional scholars on both sides of the ideological aisle, from top Reagan administration lawyer Bruce Fein to President Obama's former judicial advisor, Lawrence Tribe, raise related concerns. Namely, that ISDS tribunals have the power to review U.S. laws, regulations, executive actions, and judicial decisions. If the three arbitrators on an ISDS tribunal were to determine, say, that a U.S. Supreme Court decision was in violation of NAFTA, those three private citizens would have the power to demand that U.S. taxpayers pay compensation for that decision. It's a point that U.S. Supreme Court Chief Justice John Roberts raised in 2014, when he expressed surprise about how ISDS works. In our highly globalized world, we have become accustomed to foreign companies suing the U.S. through U.S. courts, Roberts wrote, "[b]ut even where a sovereign nation has subjected itself to suit in its own courts, it is quite another thing for it to subject itself to international arbitration." By signing a treaty that includes ISDS, he went on, a sovereign nation "permits private adjudicators to review its public policies and effectively annul the authoritative acts of its legislature, executive, and judiciary."

Liberal Democrats, meanwhile, who have been among the most vocal critics of ISDS, worry that foreign corporations will use the tool to challenge U.S. laws and regulations designed to serve the public interest—particularly financial regulations, environmental rules, and health laws. In 2013, for example, an American oil and gas company filed an ISDS claim challenging an environmental regulation in Quebec that put a moratorium

20   on fracking in rock underneath the St. Lawrence River. The oil and gas company claimed the regulation violated NAFTA by expropriating the company's future profits.

President Obama, who has broken with much of his liberal base to defend ISDS, dismisses criticism of the tool—including a few barbs from his usually staunch ally, Massachusetts Senator Elizabeth Warren—as hyperbolic "bunk" and "totally wrong." In interviews, he has repeatedly insisted that foreign corporations cannot under any circumstances use ISDS to challenge laws and regulations in the U.S. and that those who say otherwise are just "making this stuff up." (Obama made those statements nine months before TransCanada used the ISDS provisions in NAFTA to challenge his decision to cancel the Keystone.)

Part of the president's positioning may be realpolitik. It's unlikely that the powerful international business community, including the Chamber of Commerce, would support the TPP or the TTIP unless they included ISDS in some form. One former lobbyist told me that if a free trade deal did not include an investment chapter complete with ISDS, it would be considered "a total joke, it would get laughed off stage."

But another reason Obama may support the controversial mechanism is that it is, at least in theory, a major step toward one of the most intoxicating liberal promises of the last century—that an enlightened society can come together to craft a set of global rules and standards that apply to everyone equally. That's been the defining idea behind trade agreements for a generation—that together we can create a common set of global best practices, governing everything from labor and food safety

to investment protections, that will make the world a safer,
healthier, more prosperous place. ISDS is a part of that vision.
It is designed to enforce an international standard for how all
investors and corporations are treated, no matter what country
they're from, or what country they're operating in.

The problem, like all law, comes down to a question of
language. How investment chapters, bilateral investment treaties, and ISDS provisions are actually written—the words and
phrases that make their way into those hallowed documents—
matters enormously. And how those words and phrases are
ultimately interpreted by private arbitrators matters too. To put
that another way, it's not enough to simply agree that foreign
investors ought to enjoy certain property protections abroad.
There is wide consensus on that much. We've actually got to
hash out what we mean by "property." And what we mean by
"protections." And what, exactly, it looks like when a government breaches its obligation to protect that private property. If
a foreign oil company's claim on a well runs up against a local
farmer's access to clean water, who wins? And who decides who
wins?

In our hyperglobalized world, where the biggest multinational corporations are vastly wealthier and more powerful than
many of the nations where they operate, the question of how we
balance private investors' property rights with the priorities of
a public society matters most of all. ISDS—this obscure, almost
entirely ignored treaty enforcement mechanism—is at the front
and center of that debate.

Buenos Aires

When Osvaldo Guglielmino was appointed attorney general of Argentina in August 2004, he inadvertently walked into the eye of a storm. Within months of taking the job, he was facing 32 lawsuits, all filed by foreign investors and their corporations, and by 2007, nearly a dozen more had piled on. By the end of his tenure in 2010, he was staring down 47 lawsuits, collectively demanding more than $80 billion dollars in damages—a sum roughly equivalent to ten times Argentina's total sovereign reserves in 2002. All 47 lawsuits were filed under investor-state dispute settlement, or ISDS.

Having spent the previous 13 years as a judge in a federal court, Guglielmino knew the geography of Argentine law like the back of his hand. But ISDS? "It was a mystery," he told me recently, leaning onto his elbows in the office of his small law firm, perched just off the 12-lane thoroughfare that slices

through the center of Buenos Aires. "We had no experience with
it. No one did."

By the end of 2004, Guglielmino and his small team, based out of the Argentine Treasury, had learned the basics. They knew that the corporations' claims would unfold before a private, supranational tribunal. They knew that instead of the normal trappings of a court, with a judge or jury, ISDS tribunals would be manned by three private citizens, who would gather in some ad hoc conference room on the other side of the world. But as for the tricks of the trade—like how to appoint the right arbitrator or decipher how the arbitrators were likely to rule—the Argentines were in the dark. ISDS was simply too new. The lawsuits against their country represented half of all of the claims that had ever been brought against any country worldwide.

Within weeks of taking the job, Guglielmino sent up a distress flare. He begged Néstor Kirchner, who was then the president of Argentina, to hire an American law firm that had experience with ISDS. But Kirchner said the government didn't have enough money for that, so Guglielmino set off on his own. He began by prowling local universities and law firms, and asking friends for the names of their smartest former students, professors, and colleagues—anyone who knew anything about international law. "I had 29-year-olds, 30-year-olds with no experience," he recalled.

While the specific details of each case were different, nearly two dozen shared the same broad strokes. In each of those, a foreign investor or corporation, usually from the U.S. or Europe, offered a version of the same argument: Before, during, and after

24   Argentina's massive financial crisis in 2002, the government had pursued policies that violated the country's obligations under its international investment treaties. As a result, the corporations' balance sheets had suffered. They were filing ISDS claims because they wanted Argentina to compensate them for their lost profits.

Guglielmino and his scrappy new team believed that the corporations' arguments were laughable. Were the impoverished taxpayers in Argentina really going to be forced to pay compensation to multinational corporations that were hardly the biggest losers from the financial crisis? "We learned quickly," Guglielmino said. "We had to—the country depended on it." But the more they studied the rules, the less clear it was that they would win.

Guglielmino was born into a middle-class family in Pehuajó, a small city three and a half hours northwest of Buenos Aires. His father taught literature, his mother art. He and his younger brother, who died of a congenital illness as a teenager, grew up in a stable home, but came of age in the 1960s and '70s, an era of political tumult and violence in Argentina.

As a college student, Guglielmino joined the Peronist Youth Organization, a movement that fought to bring Juan Perón, the erstwhile president of Argentina, back from exile. In the early '70s, Perón served a brief, nine-month-long second term before his death in office plunged the nation into what is remembered as the Dirty War, a period of horrific state terrorism that left tens of thousands of left-wing activists and sympathizers dead. Throughout his life, Guglielmino remained committed to Peronism, a uniquely Argentine and ideologically diverse

political movement best described as nationalist populism. But
he rejected its many extreme left- and right-wing forms. To
him, Peronism is "capitalism with social mobility," he says.

As a person, Guglielmino is warm but watchful, as if always
ready to parry a blow. He pays close attention when people are
talking and leaps to his feet when he gets excited. He harbors a
deep faith in humanity's ability to do right unto each other and
laments what he sees as modern governmental and legal rules
that have been exploited by a small group of powerbrokers willing to use their leverage to enrich themselves.

Twenty-five years ago, Guglielmino, still a young lawyer in his 30s, was appointed to a federal judgeship, where his
decisions occasionally landed in the papers. In one ruling, he
refused to allow a building that had been used as a prison during
the Dirty War to be demolished. It was, he declared, a powerful
symbol of the country's unsavory legacy that must be preserved.
But for the most part, Guglielmino stayed in his lane. Untrained
in economics and with no experience abroad, he didn't second-
guess Argentina's foray into global financial markets in the '90s
or question former president Carlos Menem's predilection for
signing investment treaties. "I didn't have the slightest idea
that in those years the bilateral investment treaties were being
signed," he said, "and much less that they were giving up jurisdiction in favor of supranational courts."

When Guglielmino was first appointed to the position of
attorney general in August 2004, Argentina was still fragile
from its financial collapse two years earlier. Roving bands of
piqueteros, or protesters, were still barricading avenues in the
capital, and huge swaths of the population were still living on

26   the streets. In the 1990s, he had watched as one Peronist president, Menem, pushed the country's economy into overdrive,
and had risen to attorney general as another Peronist president,
Kirchner, attempted to save it. He was not feeling confident in
the political party he had been a member of since he was young.

"I don't know if I am a Peronist," he told reporters when he
was appointed, but he steeled himself for the job. "But I am a
patriot," he said.

Argentina's legal troubles in the 2000s trace their roots at
least as far back as 1989, when Menem, a charismatic politician whose hairline and prominent nose called to mind an
impish Richard Nixon, was elected president. Menem ran
his presidential campaign on a Peronist platform, but once in
office, he embraced the neoliberal economic theory known as
the Washington Consensus that was sweeping Latin America at
the time. Championed by the World Bank and the International
Monetary Fund, the promise of the Washington Consensus
was simple: If governments would embrace free trade, privatize
their economies, and dismantle barriers to foreign investment,
then peace and prosperity would follow.

In his first few years in power, Menem launched an ambitious effort to strip away all financial regulation, privatize nearly
all state-owned industries, and rebrand Argentina to the international investment community. With IMF cheerleaders often
just offstage, foreign investors, shuttled in from New York and
London for glitzy tours of the countryside, were eager to believe.
Over the course of the '90s, U.S. and European banks, investors, hedge funds, and corporations snapped up $186.7 billion

in Argentine bonds and purchased the country's oil fields, its airline, and its water, electricity, sewage, telephone, and gas utilities.

The boom was driven in part by Menem's embrace of what's known as the convertibility law, which established a fixed exchange rate with the U.S. dollar—one Argentine peso converted to one U.S. dollar. It was also driven by Menem's willingness to commit to sweetheart contracts and powerful investment treaties that bound Argentina to a narrow set of acceptable future actions. Many contracts, for example, included the promise that Argentina would maintain a "stable investment climate"—a line designed to assuage investors' skepticism that a country with a 150-year history of financial fecklessness had indeed reformed. If the country failed to maintain that "stable investment climate," foreign investors could sue it outside of its own courts.

Throughout the '90s, Menem's plan seemed to be working. The Argentine economy grew at an average rate of 6 percent a year, with almost no inflation, blocks of Buenos Aires's beaux arts buildings were cleaned and refurbished, and street cafés were filled with young women who had money to spend on leather coats. In 1998, at the annual IMF and World Bank meeting in Washington, President Bill Clinton and IMF chief Michel Camdessus congratulated Menem for his accomplishments. "Capitalism was the religion," recalled Guglielmino. "Adam Smith was the high priest."

But the flush times wouldn't last. Just a few months after the IMF celebration, Argentina's exports began to slump, tax revenue declined, debt piled up, and the country slipped

28   into a four-year-long recession. As financial crises rippled through the Asian and Russian markets and tipped into Brazil, Argentina's balance sheets began to bleed. Under normal circumstances, Argentina might have weakened the peso to make its exports cheaper and to lessen the burden of its loans, but, bound to the dollar by the convertibility law, it was stuck. In an attempt to keep enough cash around to pay its debts, the government instituted extreme austerity measures, begged international bondholders to cut the country some slack on repayment, and asked the IMF for help. Nothing worked.

In 2001, when Menem's second term ended and the opposition candidate from the Radical Party, Fernando de la Rúa, took power, the economy continued its relentless decline. Argentines, familiar with the signs of impending ruin, began withdrawing their money from the banks. Over the course of one month in the summer of 2001, they withdrew $5 billion, 7 percent of the total deposits in the country, and in the final days of November 2001, they pulled out $3.6 billion more. Panicked, the ministry of finance imposed a cap on the amount that people could withdraw from their accounts, but the move instead sparked fury. On December 19, a warm, austral summer day, crowds of men and women, angry that they could not access the money in their own bank accounts, swamped the streets, banged pots and pans and defied a federal curfew to cries of *que se vayan todos*—kick them all out! That night, the protests turned violent and 16 people died in clashes with police. The next day, de la Rúa resigned.

In the following weeks, the National Congress, abiding by the line of succession, appointed a series of new presidents, each of whom clattered through Casa Rosada, the Argentine

White House, like balls through a pinball machine. After de
la Rúa, there was Ramón Puerta. Then Adolfo Rodríguez Saá.
Then Eduardo Camaño. Meanwhile, the lawlessness continued. A mob broke into Congress, destroyed furniture, and lit
the curtains on fire. Protesters broke into supermarkets, scaled
walls, and police stopped showing up for work. Families moved
their beds away from the windows. Fathers slept with guns in
their hands. By the end of the month, 30 people had died in violence in the streets. Guglielmino remembers those two weeks
as an existential crisis. He recalls the German sociologist Max
Weber defining a state by its monopoly on power, and by those
terms the Argentine government had collapsed. "The streets of
Buenos Aires had no police," he said. "The state didn't exist."

On January 2, 2002, Congress appointed Eduardo Duhalde
to become the fifth president of Argentina in less than two
weeks. Unlike the others, he held on to power. Within days
of taking office, it was clear to him and other lawmakers that
they didn't have much of a choice. The convertibility law
seemed unsustainable. The debt was crushing. If they didn't
do something about it, they worried they would condemn their
society to slow-motion collapse. On January 6, Duhalde pushed
through what became known as the emergency law "[i]n order
to guarantee the operation of the National State in accordance
with available resources." The law dropped an economic bomb:
It suspended the convertibility law, halted all utility price hikes,
and put a moratorium on the enforcement of contracts until
further notice. The consequences were immediate.

By unhitching the Argentine economy from the U.S. dollar,
the law triggered a sovereign default on $81 billion in financial

30   paper. The peso plummeted in value by nearly 40 percent overnight. The GDP shrank by 11 percent, banks teetered on the
edge of insolvency, and the average income, which had peaked
at $8,500 in the 1990s, withered to $2,800. More than half the
population fell below the poverty line, and an estimated 1.2 million people moved onto the streets, where they earned the name
cartoneros after the cardboard boxes they slept in. A 59-year-
old woman who could not get her dollars out of her account set
herself on fire in the lobby of her bank. On a highway a few hours
north of Buenos Aires, a mob of hungry men and women with
kitchen knives descended on a cattle truck that had overturned
on the highway, slaughtering 22 Angus steers. Blood coated the
asphalt.

A year later, in May 2003, the economy was still in tatters
when a new president, the Peronist Néstor Kirchner, succeeded
Duhalde. Kirchner passed more political reforms in an effort,
as he put it, to buttress economic recovery "with its republican
form of government intact." By 2004, the peso began to stabilize.
Unemployment ticked down. The economy was rebounding at
last.

That's when the lawsuits started to roll in.

Four U.S. energy corporations were among the first to file ISDS
claims against Argentina. CMS, Enron, Sempra, and LG&E had
bought into the Argentine gas sector in the 1990s, at the height
of Menem's privatization craze. All four had signed contracts
with the government that, among other things, allowed them
to calculate their Argentine customers' gas bills in U.S. dollars,
and to adjust them twice a year to keep pace with the U.S. price

index. That meant that the amount they could collect in bills each month from their customers would not only remain stable, but also likely increase. It also meant that they didn't have to worry about the Argentine peso fluctuating or devaluing. On its face, it seemed like a pretty sweet deal. And, for years, it was.

But Argentina's slow descent into economic chaos in the late '90s and early 2000s changed everything. With unemployment rising and its debts ballooning, the government moved to suspend the gas companies' automatic tariff increases. (In 2002, those earlier moves were institutionalized when President Duhalde's emergency law not only unpegged the peso from the dollar, but froze utility rates at their January 2002 levels, and forbid the companies from keeping up with the U.S. price index). In 2003, when President Kirchner attempted to raise gas and electricity rates to abide by the original contracts, his efforts were blocked by court injunctions and protests. Argentines who'd lost their jobs and incomes in the economic crisis were in no mood to pay more for gas. At that point, unemployment was still topping 20 percent.

To some Argentine lawmakers, the government's action was clearly an attempt to serve the public good. They had worried that without intervention, Argentines would not be able to afford their gas bills. But to the corporations, it was an act of discrimination. CMS, Enron, Sempra, and LG&E saw the government's move not only as breach of contract but also as a violation of the terms of the U.S.-Argentina bilateral investment. In that agreement, Argentina had very clearly promised to "maintain a stable investment environment" and to "observe any obligation it may have entered into with regard

32 to investments." As a result, the gas companies demanded hundreds of millions of dollars in compensation for lost profits. By the end of 2004, they were pretty confident they'd win.

Guglielmino's team wasn't so sure. To them, the gas companies' claims seemed groundless. Breaking a contract was not the same as violating an international investment treaty, they argued. And even if it was, the Argentine government had acted well within its rights as a sovereign nation to protect its people and the security of its state during a period of extraordinary political tumult. Guglielmino argued that thousands of investment treaties worldwide, including the U.S.-Argentina agreement, were riddled with exceptions designed precisely for these kinds of scenarios—to allow governments to react to a crisis as they saw fit. If the tribunals decided against Argentina, those rulings would have huge implications for how nations all over the world, including the U.S. and the United Kingdom, might be able to react to crises of their own. The international community wouldn't stand for that, Guglielmino reasoned.

To him, the situation seemed clear. The 2002 financial crisis had been horrible. Everyone had suffered losses, and none more so than the Argentine people. In the midst of that collapse, the government had acted to protect the interests of its constituents and the security of its state. The idea that Argentine taxpayers would now be responsible for compensating foreign companies for their lost profits seemed legally untenable, set up a problematic precedent for rich, Western nations, and was morally offensive. Surely, he thought, Argentina could not lose.

A Very Short History of Investors' Rights

For the first five thousand years of human civilization, foreign investors—merchants and traders, daring enough to venture beyond the borders of their homeland—were left to their own devices. Becoming a foreigner meant becoming an outlaw, an alien in an alien land. Neighboring powers had no legal obligation to treat foreigners well and foreigners, in turn, had no claim over their hosts' laws, no standing before their judges. There was no such thing as a human right, at least in any way approaching the modern sense, and aside from basic strictures of hospitality, there was no agreed-upon standard that might prevent a wayward merchant from being relieved of his wares or riches, or his life.

Over the last 500 years, that go-it-alone culture has slowly evolved in different ways in different parts of the world. In Europe in the Middle Ages, for example, traders created a specialized law, Lex Mercatoria, that set standards governing the treatment

34 of merchants and their goods through medieval fiefdoms. In those same years, the rise of powerful guilds gave merchants the strength to enforce those standards among their own members and to organize boycotts against recalcitrant kings. In the seventeenth century, a confederation of merchant guilds, the Hanseatic League, began to provide diplomatic and military protection to convoys passing through parts of the North and Baltic Seas.

For the most part, it wasn't until the eighteenth and nineteenth centuries that any semblance of modern international law began to emerge. From a historical perspective, it was a period of extraordinary change. New forms of transportation, like steam engines and ocean liners, made it suddenly possible to travel to far-flung lands quickly, and with a reasonable expectation that one might someday return, while brand new networks of banking and insurance helped to mitigate merchants' risks and underwrite their investments. Meanwhile, the birth of modern nation-states created vast expanses of territory governed by predictable, and enforceable, laws. Instead of being dependent on one another as private guilds to set standards, enforce claims, and navigate a complex patchwork of capricious, independent powers, merchants were now in a position where they could expect complex institutions to act according to established laws.

It was in this climate that intellectuals began to pen new theories about the international rights of private investors. In the mid-1700s, the Swiss pastor and jurist Emmerich de Vattel floated the idea that a trader enjoys, by some legal transitive property, the protection of his home state, even when he is abroad. "Whoever ill-treats a citizen indirectly injures the State, which must protect that citizen," Vattel wrote. That idea—later

enshrined as diplomatic protection in international law, crept
slowly into the legal consciousness, growing and expanding as
international trade flourished.

In the late eighteenth century, governments began to
establish commissions through which private citizens could
request compensation for private property that had been seized
or destroyed during a war. One of the first such tribunals was
created in 1794 to resolve British and American citizens' loss
of property during the American Revolutionary War. Between
1829 and 1910, the U.S. entered into at least 40 more similar
agreements. While merchants and traders had no legal standing
before these early tribunals, their governments could espouse
complaints on their behalf—and they did. As the nineteenth
century wore on, governments began to convene tribunals on
behalf of citizens and investors who felt they had been bilked
abroad, even if their complaints did not arise from war.

In some ways, the emergence of these international tribunals marked an astonishing level of progress. Instead of military
powers simply waging war on behalf of their well-connected
citizens—a long-standing tradition in human civilization—they
were now choosing a peaceful means of dispute resolution. But
the story is not quite so simple. Most of these early tribunals were
riven with fraud, and while they were certainly peaceful in com-
parison to a military invasion, they were hardly diplomatic affairs.
In many cases, tribunals were used as means to force weaker
countries to repay foreign debt or to offer compensation for property seized by foreigners, whether the country in question agreed
to arbitration or not. In 1903, for example, after Venezuela refused
to repay U.S., German, British, and Italian creditors, the port of

36   Caracas was bombarded until the Venezuelans agreed to a "peaceful" arbitration, under whatever terms their creditors imposed.

The blizzard of treaties that emerged in the nineteenth and early twentieth centuries were similarly ambiguous. Written in the lilting language of friendship, they were enforced the old fashioned way: with cannons, coercion, and blood. Many of these treaties were little more than colonial contracts. The more powerful country declared one-sided import duties, enforced their own access to ports, and granted their own merchants and investors blanket privileges and protections, ensured by gunboats anchored in a harbor nearby. In 1882, when Egyptian nationalists threatened to seize British investors' assets, the British Crown arrived by ship, took over, and ran the place for 30 years. With the blessing of their home governments, chartered trading companies like the British East India Company, which maintained their own armed forces, oversaw private empires.

But if it was messy progress, it was progress nonetheless. By the early twentieth century, foreign investors had a legitimate and recognized right to private property abroad—a right that their home nations could enforce on their behalf. In 1924 the Permanent Court of International Justice formally recognized a nation-state's right to espouse its citizens' claims to private property as an "elementary principle of international law."

A Question of Sovereignty

By the mid-nineteenth century, lawyers and intellectuals began to grapple with the contradictions of this emerging legal reality. How does a government balance an obligation to respect foreign investors' private property with its own, supposedly immutable, sovereign right to act in any way it sees fit? What happens when those two forces conflict—when a sovereign nation, acting in its sovereign capacity, impinges on a foreigner's property? Two schools of thought emerged.

On one side there were the sovereign absolutists. Informed in part by the ideas of the nineteenth-century Argentine lawyer and philosopher Carlos Calvo, they argued that nations must be able to act unilaterally, according to their own customs and cultures, and in response to their own citizens' needs, without exception. If a nation chooses to seize a foreign investor's land or to nationalize an industry—well, that's its prerogative. An investor can request compensation in that nation's domestic court, but that's it. Foreign countries have no right to intervene on their investors' behalf in another sovereign nation's affairs. In 1902, the Argentine Minister of Foreign Affairs Luis María Drago doubled down on this idea, asserting that no foreign power, not even the United States, could impinge upon a nation's sovereignty to protect the interests of its citizens or to enforce the payment of debts.

On the other side were the powerful, imperial nations, which walked a more nuanced line. With regard to their own sovereignty, they too were absolutists. No foreign nation had any right to enforce its laws—or collect on behalf of its creditors—within their borders. But from their perspective, weaker countries' claims to sovereignty were subject to debate. Under the banner of enforcing the rules of a "civilized" society, U.S. and European governments reserved the right to enforce their citizens' property rights within "less civilized" nations' borders. Between 1820 and 1914, Britain militarily intervened in Latin

38 America on behalf of its investors at least 40 times—that is, until the U.S., armed with the Monroe Doctrine, began asserting itself in the role of enforcer in its own backyard.

By the early twentieth century, international law was still ambiguous on the issue. In the wake of mass nationalizations of private, American-owned ranches in Mexico in 1938, U.S. Secretary of State Cordell Hull wrote to the Mexican government demanding "prompt, adequate, and effective" compensation for the American citizens' seized property. As a sovereign nation, Mexico may have the power to seize that land, Hull wrote, but that did not exempt it from the "ancient belief" in "an unchanging and rigid concept of property rights."

The Mexican ambassador to the U.S., meanwhile, defended his country's expropriations on the grounds that the Mexican government, as a sovereign nation, had a legitimate right to act on behalf of its people. The Americans' ranches had been seized for a program of agrarian reform, necessary to advance the well-being of Mexican citizens, he explained. "On the one hand, there are weighed the claims of justice and the improvement of a whole people, and on the other hand, the purely pecuniary interests of some individuals," he wrote. He added that the "future of the nation could not be halted by the impossibility of paying immediately the value of properties belonging to a small number of foreigners who seek only a lucrative end."

Mexico ended up compensating the American landowners for their ranches, but the intellectual standoff underscored an unanswered question on the international stage: When an investor's right to private property bumps up against a sovereign nation's decision to act on behalf of itself or its people, who wins?

Must a nation always pay compensation for seizing a foreign-   39
er's private property, and if so, under what circumstances? How
much? And who decides? Attempts to answer those questions
would define the next 75 years of international investment law.

The Capitalist Magna Carta

Beginning in the mid-twentieth century, economists and intellectuals in Europe and the U.S. seized on the idea of a multilateral
investment treaty. The idea was to establish, once and for all, a set
of global rules for how investors and their property must be treated
around the world. While each of these proposals was slightly different, all echoed and underscored the message in Hull's letter: If a
nation seizes or destroys a foreign national's property, it must provide prompt, adequate, and effective compensation for that seizure.

In 1944, a handful of the most prominent economic minds
of a generation included language designed to protect foreign
investors' property rights in the proposal for the International
Trade Organization, which was never ratified. In the 1950s,
a group of European nations that would later become the
Organization for Economic Cooperation and Development tried
again. In 1957, *Time* magazine called one such proposal "the
Capitalist Magna Carta." It included a provision allowing foreign investors to demand the creation of a dispute settlement
tribunal. Only unlike the tribunals that had risen to prominence
on the international stage in the nineteenth and early twentieth
centuries, these would not involve an investor's home country.
Under this proposal, an investor could sit at the arbitration table
directly with a sovereign nation, without involving his home

40   government, and without first exhausting the judicial options in his host country's court system. It was a revolutionary idea.

Advocates sold this new multilateral investment treaty as a win-win for everyone. Investors, they argued, would benefit from beefed-up property protections and developing countries would benefit from an uptick in foreign investment, as wealthy investors and corporations felt more comfortable building their operations abroad. Powerful governments, meanwhile, would benefit from being relieved from the obligation to intervene diplomatically or militarily on their investors' behalf. That, in turn, would help safeguard smaller nations' sovereignty, discourage wars over commercial issues, and buttress world peace. "I am convinced," the World Bank President George Woods said triumphantly at the time, "that those...who adopt as their national policy a welcome [environment] for international investment—and that means, to mince no words about it, giving foreign investors a fair opportunity to make attractive profits—will achieve their development objectives more rapidly than those who do not."

The era of decolonization in the 1950s and '60s raised the temperature on the issue. As dozens of newly independent states emerged, throwing off their colonial yokes, they were keen to showcase their newfound sovereignty—and often did so by nationalizing foreign investors' property. Instances of expropriation spiked from the Middle East to Latin America—along with tensions between developing nations and the major economic powers, which often could not resist intervening on their investors' behalf. In 1954, for example, the young Argentine revolutionary Che Guevara happened to be in Guatemala as newly elected leftist leader Jacobo Arbenz Guzmán attempted

to reclaim unused land from the powerful banana company
United Fruit. But Guzmán was ousted in a CIA-engineered coup
designed to protect the well-connected fruit company's interests. Guevara later remembered it as a radicalizing moment.

Meanwhile, the harder the Europeans worked to pass a multilateral investment treaty, the more vehemently developing nations
opposed it. Miguel Cuaderno, the governor of the Philippines' central bank, told the *New York Times* that the Europeans' proposed
treaty amounted to foreign control through bureaucratic means.
Instead, a group of nearly two dozen developing nations rallied
behind the so-called New International Economic Order, which,
echoing the "sovereign absolutism" of the century-old Calvo
Doctrine, sanctified a nation's total and unilateral control over
everything within its borders. A sovereign nation, they declared,
could do whatever it wanted on its own soil—even if that meant
expropriating a foreign investor's property without compensating anyone. The United Nations later passed a series of resolutions
asserting nations' "permanent sovereignty over natural resources."

The developing nations' revolt in the 1970s succeeded in ending the effort to impose a multilateral investment treaty. But that
was hardly the end of the story.

Let's Sign a BIT

In the 1940s, '50s, and '60s, as developing nations battled proposals for a multilateral investment treaty, they quietly embraced
the ideas embedded in them—just on a smaller scale. Beginning
in 1959, developing countries began signing bilateral investment
treaties, or BITs, that were nearly identical, in both language and

42   spirit, to the Europeans' multilateral version—all the way down to the promise that nations agree to compensate foreign investors for acts of expropriation. The only difference between BITs and the failed multilateral versions was that with the bilateral treaties, countries bound themselves to just one other investment partner.

For the most part, these BITs were vague on details. Unlike some of the multilateral investment treaty proposals, they did not outline how an investor might demand arbitration with his host country. Nor did they explain how a foreign investor would go about demanding compensation for an act of expropriation, or how an investor and a government would arrive at the appropriate amount of compensation. In 1965, some of those logistical questions were answered when the World Bank established the International Centre for Settlement of Investment Disputes, or ICSID, offering rules that would govern arbitrations between foreign investors and their host states. Later, the United Nations Commission on International Trade Law, or UNCITRAL, set up rules for international investor-state arbitration, too. In 1969, the first BIT that specifically included ISDS—thus binding a nation to arbitration, should it impinge on a foreigner investor's rights— found its way onto the books. It was the beginning of an era.

Historians today argue over why developing nations, which so vehemently opposed proposals for a multilateral investment treaty, were keen to accept nearly identical provisions in BITs. José Alvarez, a professor of law at New York University, links nations' willingness to sign BITs to promotions by the World Bank, the International Monetary Fund, and to the politics of neoliberalism that began to take hold in the late '70s and '80s. Andrew Guzman, the dean of University of Southern California Gould School of

Law, describes it in terms of a prisoners' dilemma. Developing
countries, in need of foreign capital, were willing to submit to
wealthy countries' demands if it meant they would receive preferential trade terms over their neighbors, he explains. In the 1960s
and '70s, powerful nations regularly offered more favorable trade
treatment to nations that did their geopolitical or military bid-
ding. For example, after the Chinese Communist Revolution of
1949, the U.S. offered sweeter deals to Taiwan, Korea, and Japan
than to other developing nations in an effort to keep those economies in the capitalist fold. During the Vietnam War, the U.S.
extended that preferential treatment to other Southeast Asian
nations for the same reason. In that environment, developing
nations might have been eager to submit to otherwise unsavory
provisions, if it meant outmaneuvering a competitor.

Meanwhile, Rachel Wellhausen, an assistant professor of
government at the University of Texas at Austin, and the author
of *The Shield of Nationality: When Governments Break Contracts
with Foreign Firms*, argues that developing nations' apparently
contradictory behavior makes more sense in light of the fact
that almost without exception, they couldn't have known what
they were getting into. For the first decades after many BITs were
signed, ISDS was virtually never used. Even after the World Bank
established the ICSID in 1965, it was unclear to most government
officials and international lawyers how, exactly, it would work.
There's very little in the historical record to indicate that either
ICSID or UNCITRAL were designed with the expectation that
there would be a massive influx of new ISDS claims under BITs.
It wasn't until 1972 that ICSID registered its first ISDS dispute,
and in its first 15 years of existence, it registered a grand total of

44   seven cases. The legal literature during this period treated ISDS as a strange duck. Lawyers wondered if it was even legal under international law for a country to pre-consent to arbitration with a private investor.

In that environment, Wellhausen explains, signing a BIT did not have an obvious downside. "You hear these stories where a president or a country's leader was eager, for political reasons, to be able to point at something positive that came out of a diplomatic meeting," said Wellhausen. "So he would just tell his foreign minister, 'Let's sign a BIT.' And they would sign it."

The U.S. was slow to come around to the idea of BITs, along with their ISDS provisions, in part because throughout the 1960s and '70s, U.S. foreign policy took a more hands-on approach. If a foreign leader was unfriendly to American businesses, it was generally preferred that he be removed from the equation and replaced with someone friendlier to America's interests. Congressional investigations, judges, and historians have found former Secretary of State Henry Kissinger's fingerprints on efforts to remove and replace socialist leaders from Chile to Cyprus. In part hoping to move away from that heavy-handed strategy, President Jimmy Carter pushed the U.S. State Department in the later 1970s to embrace BITs. In the early 1980s, the Reagan administration launched the first U.S. BIT program.

The U.S. arrived just on time for the global party. Between 1959, when the first BIT was signed, and 1989, countries had only committed to about 385 BITs total. By the 1990s, signing them had become vogue, as trade negotiators began folding BITs—including their ISDS provisions—into chapters of larger, multilateral, and sector-specific trade agreements, like

the Association of Southeast Asian Nations Comprehensive
Investment Agreement and the Energy Charter Treaty, linking
oil and gas producing nations and the European Union. Between
1990 and 2000, the number of investment treaties worldwide
leapt to 1,857, and by the start of 2016 there were more than 3,271.

NAFTA, which established one of the largest free-trade areas
in history between the U.S., Canada, and Mexico, was a particularly important tipping point. It marked the first time ever that
an international treaty between close investment partners—two
of them well-developed, complex democracies—included all the
provisions of a BIT as well as ISDS. The move not only allowed
American and Canadian investors to challenge Mexico outside of
its shaky judicial system, it also allowed investors from all three
signatory countries to challenge the U.S. and Canada outside
of their robust and reliable courts. That was unprecedented—a
watershed in the history of investors' rights.

But in the early '90s, it was on almost nobody's radar. That's
partly because, even when NAFTA was ratified in 1994, ISDS had
so rarely been used. In the previous three decades, there were
only public records for about two dozen claims, and records
show that most corporations' legal arms weren't aware of the
existence of ISDS. In 1992, even as Ross Perot famously begged
Congress not to ratify NAFTA—arguing that it would create a
"giant sucking sound" of American jobs going to Mexico—he
never mentioned ISDS. It was not litigated in the pages of the
New York Times. It was not debated on the nightly news. It did
not enter the public discussion at all. In January 1995, with
President Clinton as its champion and Republicans backing it in
Congress, NAFTA went into effect. This almost forgotten legal
provision would forever change the legal landscape abroad.

The Battle of La Pedrera

On a warm day in September 1993, four months before NAFTA would go into effect, Grant Kesler, the white-haired CEO of Metalclad Corporation, a small industrial firm with offices in Newport Beach, California, made a decision he would come to regret. He agreed to buy a Mexican waste management company called Coterin.

Coterin owned a site called La Pedrera in an arid corner of San Luis Potosí, a sun-soaked Mexican state. While Kesler had no experience building or maintaining hazardous waste facilities, and no operations abroad—Metalclad had spent decades in asbestos removal in the U.S.—he and his executives saw Mexico as a ripe market. At the time, the country did not have enough hazardous waste landfills, and both federal and state authorities, including the recently elected governor of San Luis Potosí, Horacio Sánchez Unzueta, had explicitly encouraged foreign investment in the sector.

Still, there were some red flags. In late 1990 and 1991, two years before Kesler purchased the company, Coterin had made enemies in La Pedrera. It had dumped roughly 30,000 tons of hazardous waste—a toxic mixture of old paint, batteries, expired drugs, and industrial sludge—into unlined ditches at the site and then left the sludge there uncovered for months, infuriating many of the 6,500 people who lived nearby. The locals worried that the groundwater, which they relied on through wells, would be contaminated; that wind from the site would cause birth defects; and that the population of desert animals that they used for food would be degraded. Community leaders from Guadalcázar, the town nearest La Pedrera, wrote angry letters to state and federal agencies demanding that Coterin's site be cleaned and closed. When Coterin retroactively applied for a permit to construct a waste facility at La Pedrera, the Guadalcázar city council refused—twice. Local leaders later recruited the support of environmental non-profits, including Greenpeace, to battle on their behalf.

In the fall of '93, as Kesler was gearing up to buy Coterin, Metalclad lawyers also noted a couple potential problems. While Coterin had all the state and federal building, land use, and operating permits it needed to construct a new waste plant, it was missing two things: Governor Sánchez Unzueta's authorization of the project and a municipal permit from the city council in Guadalcázar. In its contract to purchase Coterin, Metalclad noted those omissions. The majority of Metalclad's payment to Coterin, the contract read, would be deferred until after the governor "has authorized to proceed with the construction" and after "the Municipal permit for the building of the

48   aforementioned confinement has been obtained by Coterin, or
      as the case may be, definitive judgment...that allows [the com-
      pany] to legally proceed with the building of such confinement."

In October 1993, Governor Sánchez Unzueta offered his qualified endorsement for the project, saying he would back Metalclad's landfill at La Pedrera, so long as the company worked with the local community and the state university and "secured their support." At that point, even without the municipal permit, Kesler forged ahead, and Metalclad formally purchased Coterin. "We felt that the key to the broader political support was not direct to the people," Kesler told the journalist Bill Moyers years later. "And every advisor that I had in Mexico told me that if the governor supports the project, you don't have to worry about that local community." It was a fateful decision.

Within months of beginning construction, a state and local rebellion against Metalclad began to rise. Community leaders in Guadalcázar reiterated their demand that La Pedrera be cleaned and closed immediately, and in January 1994, Pedro Medellin, the head of the environmental office in the state, issued a report expressing doubts about whether the site was environmentally sound for a hazardous waste site.

Bracing themselves for public backlash, both Governor Sánchez Unzueta and Metalclad issued statements. The governor, distancing himself from the project, reminded Metalclad that "it is absolutely necessary to have the agreement of the people of Guadalcázar, who have repeatedly expressed their opposition in the media." Metalclad, meanwhile, extended an olive branch. In an advertisement published in Spanish in local papers, the company promised to clean up Coterin's mess. Left unaddressed, those open sludge pits "may post a great danger to the health of the inhabitants," the advertisement read. Metalclad's new facility would be state of the art, they promised.

The company's overture fell flat. Over the next year, state health officials, citing controversial studies, expressed concern that hazardous waste from the site could lead to miscarriages, malformations in children, and higher rates of disease, stoking local fears. Someone scrawled *Fuera Metalclad*—Get out, Metalclad—on a wall in Guadalcázar. Still, Metalclad pushed forward with the construction and the federal government of Mexico, cognizant of the need for more hazardous waste sites in the country, encouraged the company to endure.

In March 1995, after more than a year of construction, Metalclad opened its new hazardous waste facility at La Pedrera. At the launch ceremony, local protesters mobbed the entrance of the plant, blocked the movement of buses carrying visiting officials, and demanded that Metalclad leave. State police had to be called in to keep the peace. Metalclad was stymied. In an effort to begin operations, the businessmen entered into negotiations with federal authorities, eventually agreeing to invest in cleaning and remediating the damage that Coterin had left at the site, in exchange for increasing the permitted capacity of the facility by a factor of ten.

When the local community heard about the pact between Metalclad and the feds, they rebelled. Just as it had with Coterin, the Guadalcázar city council denied Metalclad a construction permit. It then filed a lawsuit challenging the company's agreement with the feds, demanding that no waste be moved to the

50   site until the dispute was resolved. Kesler was incensed. He brought a counter lawsuit against Guadalcázar for refusing to issue a permit. How could the federal authorities support the project while simultaneously allowing it to be thwarted by state and local officials?

But it was a losing battle for Metalclad. By the summer of 1995, Leonel Ramos, mayor of Guadalcázar, with public opinion firmly on his side, announced that the people had won. "There is nothing in the world," he crowed to a regional newspaper, "that can open the landfill due to the community's opposition."

First of Its Kind

Metalclad's saga in La Pedrera seemed to have all the bones of a Hollywood drama. There was the impoverished local community that banded together to fight the construction of a hazardous landfill, and the bombastic politician, Governor Sánchez Unzueta, struggling on their behalf. Lawsuits had been filed, protesters had amassed. But then there was a plot twist.

In January 1995, just two months before Metalclad announced the grand opening of the La Pedrera site, NAFTA went into effect. The treaty gave Metalclad a powerful new tool. Armed with that treaty's ISDS provisions, it no longer had to worry about the two lawsuits wending their way through the Mexican judicial system. It didn't have to negotiate a solution with the people of Guadalcázar. It suddenly had the ability to go above the heads of the Mexican judges entirely: By simply filing an ISDS claim, a private, supranational tribunal would be called in to sort it all out.

On October 2, 1996, Metalclad filed the first-ever ISDS claim under NAFTA, demanding that Mexico pay $90 million in compensation for the "arbitrary and malicious" actions of Governor Sánchez Unzueta and other officials in the Mexican government. "This case exemplifies the very reasons why the Investment Chapter of the NAFTA was enacted—why standards of treatment, including due process and fair and equitable treatment; and why strict criteria for expropriation, including payment of full and fair compensation—are codified within," the company's lawyers wrote in a statement announcing the suit. Metalclad claimed that the actions of Mexico's local, state, and federal officials had been so egregiously unfair they amounted to an expropriation of the company's property.

Among Mexicans, Metalclad's ISDS claim was met with confusion and outrage. How could a private, foreign corporation challenge the democratic decision of a state and local government? Did the people of Guadalcázar and San Luis Potosí have a democratic right to both protest and withhold a permit from a project they disagreed with? How was the Guadalcázar city council's decision to withhold a permit a violation of an *international* treaty?

At the state and local level, one main frustration seemed to be aimed at the fact that an American company had the power to invoke a special, supranational tribunal outside of the Mexican judicial system. If Metalclad had a complaint with state and local government decisions, why shouldn't it have to file a lawsuit in a state or local court, like everyone else? Another frustration was aimed at how this supranational system worked. Under ISDS,

52   foreign investors enter arbitrations with the federal govern-
     ment—and the federal government only. That not only allowed
     Metalclad to do an end-run around Mexican courts, it allowed
     them to cut the people of Guadalcázar and San Luis Potosí out
     of the dispute resolution equation entirely. At ISDS tribunals,
     state and local authorities don't even have a seat at the table.

At the federal level, Mexico's lawyers seemed most concerned with the lawsuit's implications for Mexico's federalized
government. They dismissed the idea that a local government's
decision to deny a company a permit can be considered an "expropriation" of a foreign investor's property under an international
treaty. For one, the locals had been willing to grant the company
a permit to build a waste facility—just not a *hazardous* waste
facility. For another, the government wasn't denying Metalclad a
permit so that it could allow another, Mexican company to build
a facility instead. The locals had been clear that they would not
only fight Metalclad's hazardous waste facility; they would fight
any hazardous waste facility operated by *any* company.

In its court filing, Mexico's lawyers seemed ready to dis-
miss Metalclad's argument as downright spurious. Metalclad,
Mexico argued, was merely attempting "to recover losses caused
of its own making." More generally, Mexico's lawyers argued
that the premise of Metalclad's claim established a dangerous
precedent. If the actions of state and local officials in San Luis
Potosí counted as an international treaty violation, it would
open the floodgates to countless more claims. The officials in
San Luis Potosí and Guadalcázar had perhaps behaved in ways
that were frustrating and petty, but isn't that par for the course
in a democracy? In the years leading up to Metalclad's battle over

La Pedrera, the Mexicans pointed out, the U.S. Environmental
Protection Agency had attempted to build nine hazardous waste
facilities across the country. All nine had been thwarted by local
protests despite federal efforts to get them built.

Metalclad's lawyers were unmoved. They felt that the company had been abused, manipulated, and discriminated against
in Mexico. They wanted compensation not only for their investment but for their lost future profits. Why had federal authorities
encouraged Metalclad to build the site at La Pedrera, even as
state officials were blocking it? Why had other companies in the
past not been required to receive a municipal permit from the
Guadalcázar city council? Why were other companies allowed to
build hazardous waste sites in other parts of the country?

Metalclad's lawyers pointed out that when a sovereign
nation signs an international treaty, all levels of government are bound by its obligations, whether they like it or not.
Massachusetts or Minnesota can't simply pass a law or regulation that violates the U.S. government's treaty obligations. An
international treaty that exempted state and local authorities
from compliance would be very weak indeed. "It's very often in
a federalized state that a subsidiary government will put up its
hand and create difficulties for you," explained Geoff Cowper, a
Canadian lawyer who was counsel to Metalclad in a related case.
"If you don't have the guarantee that they will act according to
due process, then you really have a limited guarantee."

News of Metalclad's ISDS claim against Mexico rippled through
the international investment community, drawing sharp
attention particularly in the U.S. and Canada. It wasn't just

54   that it was the first ISDS claim under NAFTA; it was also that
      Metalclad's case was unique. In the 35 years that ISDS had been
      included in treaties up to that point, companies had filed ISDS
      claims only rarely and generally only after a government out-
      right seized or destroyed a foreign company's assets. Investors
      had used ISDS to ensure that a third party determined the value
      of its seized or destroyed asset. They had never used ISDS to
      determine whether its asset had been seized or destroyed in the
      first place.

      Metalclad's claim broke that mold. At the time that the
      company filed its case, Mexico had not seized or destroyed any
      of Metalclad's property. Instead, the company was arguing that
      the collective actions of state and local officials, by refusing to
      issue permits or advocating against the project, amounted to
      an expropriation. Mexico *might as well have* seized or destroyed
      its property, since the effect on Metalclad's bottom line was the
      same.

      Metalclad's argument resonated with some observ-
      ers. Surely, the definition of expropriation must reflect the
      modern world, where large, powerful governments oversee a
      complex latticework of state and local rules and regulations. If
      an investor puts money in a mobile taco stand and finds later
      that the government has passed a law banning mobile taco
      stands, the government hasn't technically seized or destroyed
      the investor's property. But that investor still loses something
      substantial. "We're not talking about the government taking
      his land or physical assets, but it's still a real loss," explained
      Cowper. "Depending on context and intent it may breach other
      protections or indeed be an expropriation measure."

But lawyers, government officials, and activists also saw a red flag. Metalclad's argument seemed to tread on dangerous ground. How do you make sure that a broader definition of expropriation does not erode a government's legitimate right to regulate? Surely, a municipal government has the right to determine whether it will permit or ban food trucks just as it has the right to decide whether it will issue a permit for a hazardous waste facility. If a city's decision to deny a foreign company a permit, after the federal government has already provided permission, counts as an international treaty violation, then that has major implications for state and local rule.

The Metalclad case fueled what would become an intellectual civil war in the international environmental and human rights community (see Chapter 7). Under what circumstances should state and local communities have total control over what happens in their backyards? When do broader, global problems, like human trafficking or environmental degradation, require that decisions by federal and international bodies ultimately triumph over local desires? Mexico, for example, was in need of more state-of-the-art hazardous waste facilities. Without them, Mexican industrialists had been dumping their hazardous waste in unlined pits or paying to truck it thousands of miles to the U.S. From an environmental standpoint, should the 6,500 local residents of the region surrounding La Pedrera have been allowed to thwart what was arguably an environmental net-positive from a global perspective? Do such cost-benefit analyses even have a place in discussions where local communities are concerned, rightly or wrongly, about a project's impact on their children's health?

Hail Mary

In August 2000, the ISDS tribunal, which consisted of three prominent experts in international investment law, Sir Elihu Lauterpacht, Benjamin R. Civiletti, and José Luis Siqueiros, issued a terse, 35-page decision, siding with Metalclad on every point.

The decision began with the low-hanging fruit. In 1997, a year after Metalclad filed its claim against Mexico, Governor Sánchez Unzueta had issued an executive decree converting the entire La Pedrera site to a state environmental cactus reserve. That action, the arbitrators decided, clearly amounted to an expropriation of Metalclad's property, and therefore required compensation from the Mexican government. The tribunal did not question the governor's right to declare a protected reserve; the issue was only that the government ought to pay compensation for indirectly seizing Metalclad's land and facility. They ordered Mexico to pay Metalclad $16.7 million—what it spent on buying Coterin, the construction, and accrued interest—in compensation. From a legal perspective, that part of the decision was mostly uncontroversial.

But then, the tribunal's decision got more contentious. The three arbitrators went on to determine that even if Governor Sánchez Unzueta *hadn't* expropriated Metaclad's property by declaring La Pedrera a cactus reserve, the state and local officials' collective actions were enough to constitute an expropriation in their own right. In fact, the arbitrators decided, *any* act by *any* government official that results in even a *partial* loss of a company's "reasonably-to-be-expected" profits amounts to an expropriation—and therefore warrants compensation. The

arbitrators offered a definition. "Expropriation under NAFTA,"
they wrote,

> includes not only open, deliberate and acknowledged takings
> of property, such as outright seizure or formal or obligatory
> transfer of title in favour of the host State, but also covert
> or incidental interference with the use of property which has
> the effect of depriving the owner, in whole or in significant
> part, of the use or reasonably-to-be-expected economic ben-
> efit of property even if not necessarily to the obvious benefit
> of the host State.

It was an extraordinary decision. By that definition, it
seemed feasible that any new law or regulation that impinged
even partially on a company's future profits—its "reasonably-
to-be-expected economic benefit of property"—could amount
to an expropriation under NAFTA. The decision seemed to open
the floodgates for endless new ISDS claims, and endless money
that governments would have to pay to companies in compensation for all kinds of supposedly "expropriatary" acts.

Mexico's lawyers were blindsided, but the shock was not
limited to Mexico City. In Washington and Ottawa, government lawyers began to sound the alarm. The Metalclad decision,
they argued, stepped way outside the intended scope of NAFTA,
but what could they do about it? Under ISDS, there is no way to
appeal a tribunal's decision. Decisions are final and binding and
must be carried out by the country as if they were that country's
own law. Faced with that dead end, Mexico filed for an arbitral
annulment before the Supreme Court of British Columbia on the

58   grounds that the decision of the ISDS tribunal, which had physically convened in Vancouver, was so egregious that it violated *Canadian* law. While such challenges have since become common, at the time, it felt like the legal equivalent of a Hail Mary.

On the day of the hearing, television camera crews and protesters gathered on the steps of the Vancouver courthouse. Lawyers from Mexico, the U.S., and Canada were all present, as were representatives from the province of Quebec, which weighed in on Mexico's behalf, on the grounds that the case represented an unsanctioned shift in power from provinces and states to a centralized authority.

Months later, British Columbia Supreme Court Justice David Franklin Tysoe issued a 30-page decision. It was clear, he wrote, that San Luis Potosí Governor Sánchez Unzueta's decree making La Pedrera a cactus reserve amounted to an expropriation of Metalclad's property. As for the bigger questions—whether the Mexican officials' actions blocking the project amounted to expropriation, and whether the tribunal's definition of expropriation had gone too far—were outside the scope of his authority, he wrote. The Metalclad tribunal's decision stood.

The case marked the beginnng of a new era of vast and creative new ISDS claims. When could a foreign investor use ISDS? What constituted an expropriation? International lawyers found themselves suddenly in the center of the legal equivalent of the Wild West.

Panning for Gold

After a six-year stint with the Canadian government, Todd Weiler was looking to do something new. The young lawyer had heard that Barry Appleton, an eccentric and dedicated attorney who ran Appleton & Associates, was doing interesting work with the investment chapter in NAFTA, but Weiler didn't know much about it. Even after reading the chapter himself, he didn't get it. "I just didn't see it," Weiler said recently. But after Weiler sat down with Appleton, that changed. "He explained that it could be used in a totally different way than anyone thought," Weiler said. "It was like having scales fall off your eyes." In 1997, Weiler got a job with Appleton's firm.

The business model at Appleton & Associates, a boutique, Toronto-based firm, relied on the staff drumming up new business—sifting through newspapers in search of

60   international legal or regulatory standoffs that might violate NAFTA's investment protections. If any of them found a promising case, they were supposed to reach out to whatever company was affected and try to convince them to make an ISDS claim. But it was tough going. At the time, most CEOs didn't know anything about ISDS. Most had never heard about the investment chapter in NAFTA. As late as 1999, even the United Nations Conference on Trade and Development was unclear about the utility of ISDS. In a report, UNCTAD experts puzzled over when the mechanism should be used, under what circumstances, and to what end. To encourage his staff, Appleton paid $500 to anyone who found a potential case, $500 more for snagging an interview with the company that had been affected, and another $500 if it signed on as a client.

Still, for years, Weiler remembers going to conferences, talking to trade lawyers about ISDS, and getting blank stares in return. "I would describe what I was doing and their eyes would glaze over. 'It's not commercial arbitration? It's not contract law?' There was confusion," he said. At one conference, Weiler remembers meeting John Jackson, the founding director of the Institute of International Economic Law and one of the creators of the intellectual framework of the World Trade Organization dispute settlement procedures. Jackson's book on international trade law was practically required reading for trade specialists. If anyone would know about ISDS, which, by that point in the late '90s, was being included in nearly every new trade deal, it would be him, Weiler thought. "But I told John Jackson what I was doing, and it didn't register for him either," he said. "No one was paying attention."

When the NAFTA text was first negotiated in the late 1980s, officials in the George H. W. Bush administration lobbied hard to include ISDS in it. U.S. and Canadian investors operating in Mexico would need a way to avoid capricious Mexican courts, they argued. Pat Mulloy, who was chief international counsel for the Senate banking committee during the Bush I administration, remembers folks from the U.S. Trade Representative's office coming in and complaining about all the corruption in then Mexican President Carlos Salinas's government. "USTR didn't want the Mexican courts deciding whether [a U.S. investor's property] had been expropriated," said Mulloy, who later served as an assistant secretary at the Department of Commerce under Clinton. "That was the way it was talked about."

At the time, Mulloy and his colleagues didn't think much of it. ISDS had so rarely been used that it didn't seem like a big deal. They also didn't consider the possibility that it could be used against the U.S. Given everything Mulloy and his colleagues knew about the mechanism—that it was primarily a means to get compensation for acts of expropriation in developing countries—the prospect that a Mexican or Canadian company would use ISDS to challenge U.S. government actions just didn't seem likely. Why would the U.S. ever expropriate a foreign company's property?

Mulloy and his colleagues also didn't foresee a huge amount of foreign investment coming to the U.S. from other countries. For as long as anyone could remember, foreign direct investment had been largely a one-way street: Wealthy, Western nations like the U.S. were "capital exporters" and poor, developing nations were "capital importers." But in the mid-1990s,

62   that shifted. The Soviet Union collapsed, the Cold War ended, the World Trade Organization was established, globalization exploded, the Internet came in, and suddenly, investors from all over the world were investing everywhere else. Almost overnight, Western nations were importing almost as much capital from developing nations as they were exporting to them. The percentage of foreign direct investment originating outside the traditional economic powers quadrupled between the '90s and late 2000s.

It was during this same time period that the number of new investment treaties began to explode. Over the course of the 1990s, more than 170 countries signed more than a thousand new BITs and other investment treaties. Even developing countries were getting in on the action. China signed 120 BITs. Egypt signed 100. Cuba signed more than 60. By the end of the decade, the number of BITs between two developing countries represented nearly a quarter of all BITs worldwide.

All of those new treaties, taken collectively, had the effect of creating a vast web—a "spaghetti bowl," as the economist Jagdish Bhagwati has called it—of investor protections that spanned the globe. It wasn't exactly a formal, multilateral treaty on investment as the Europeans had pushed for in the '40s and '50s (see Chapter 2), but it did provide a base level of protection for investors in most countries. If an investor's own government did not have an investment treaty with the country where he was operating, chances were that another country did and he could restructure his corporation to take advantage of it, a strategic move that earned a new name: treaty shopping. By the late 1990s, it began to dawn on CEOs that these BITs and investment

chapters in treaties like NAFTA and the Energy Charter could be   63
very valuable indeed.

Meanwhile, a legal and scholarly ecosystem began to sprout
around ISDS. Law schools across the U.S. and Europe began
offering classes on the mechanism—something that would
have been unheard of just a few years earlier—and newly minted
specialists began penning articles, spreading the word about
the potential power of the tool. Between 2000 and 2010, most
major corporate law firms in the U.S. launched ISDS boutiques
under their roofs, drawing some of the most creative and ambitious legal minds. After all, ISDS was an exciting, dynamic
specialty of law, and virtually untested. No one knew what the
boundaries of investment protections in treaties were, so there
was infinite potential, infinite space for creativity. What *exactly*
did these BITs and investment chapters promise? When did a
regulation amount to an expropriation? And what constituted
an expropriation in the first place?

"I Know It When I See It"

Because all of the BITs and investment chapters had been ratified in an era before they were the subject of litigation, they
were, almost without exception, written in extraordinarily
vague terms. They used the "soaring overtures of diplomacy,"
explained one negotiator who worked in the State Department
in the '80s, rather than the "staccato precision" of a legal document. Most early investment treaties were just five or six
pages long and did not bother with fine print at all. Most did
not describe what constituted an investment, offer a definition

64   of expropriation, or include any language whatsoever protecting a country's right to regulate in the public interest. In 2000,
William Rogers, the former secretary of state under Richard
Nixon, described the language in BITs as "dazzlingly abstract"
and "maddeningly imprecise as to the substantive legal standard to be applied by the tribunal."

But if BITs and investment chapters were vague, they were
similar in their vagueness. Because the vast majority of investment treaties were ratified around the same time, countries
borrowed from each other's texts. Entire paragraphs, phrases,
and sections were often simply copied and pasted from one
document to the next. "You might see 'fair' instead of 'just,' or
something like that," said William Burke-White, a professor and
deputy dean of the University of Pennsylvania Law School and an
expert on ISDS. "But they were overwhelmingly similar in both
language and content." For example, in almost every investment
treaty on the books then (and now), countries are obligated to
provide foreign investors with "fair and equitable treatment."
They are also required to offer "full protection and security," to
refrain from behaving in ways that are "arbitrary or discriminatory," and to pay compensation after "acts of expropriation." But
what do those phrases really mean under a legal microscope?

In the late '90s and early 2000s, lawyers like Weiler and
Appleton were just beginning to explore the boundaries of
that language. What was the legal definition of "fair"? When,
precisely, did a federal government slip from behaving like
a normal democracy to behaving "arbitrarily"? In 2004, two
prominent arbitrators, L. Yves Fortier and Stephen L. Drymer,

mused over the slippery definition of expropriation. From a legal perspective, the term was so abstract, they wrote, that the effort to define it recalled former U.S. Supreme Court justice Potter Stewart's struggle to define pornography: "I know it when I see it." (A decade later, much of the language in investment treaties has remained opaque. In July 2014, a group of 120 professors of law and legal theory wrote a letter to the U.S. Trade Representative's office complaining that phrases were often so vague that tribunals could feasibly interpret all kinds of legitimate regulatory actions as a treaty violation demanding compensation.)

It was in this Wild West legal environment that the number of ISDS claims began to explode. In the 35 years between 1960 and 1995, multinational corporations brought about three dozen ISDS claims total. Between 1996 and 2005, there was a 14-fold increase, and by the end of 2015, there were more than 700. And it was just volume. The claims weren't anything like what Mulloy, the former Clinton trade official, and his colleagues had expected. For one, the U.S. and other developing countries were finding themselves on the receiving end of a growing number claims. Of the 14 NAFTA cases in the late '90s and 2000, four were against the U.S. and six were against Canada. And for another, the claims seemed to have very little to do with a government outright expropriating or nationalizing a foreign company's property—at least by any traditional definition of those terms. "We just did not see that they could use ISDS to challenge the ability of our states to regulate by suggesting that our state and local governments had impaired the

66   value of their investment," said Mulloy, before offering a dead-
pan reaction. "So, yes. That was a surprise."

Todd Weiler was on the front lines of this legal expedition. What
kinds of claims would tribunals accept? How would they calculate compensation? Shortly after taking the job at Appleton
& Associates, Weiler joined his colleagues in representing S.D.
Myers, an American waste disposal company, in a claim against
Canada. The company's business model was built largely on
processing and disposing of polychlorinated biphenyl, or PCB,
a toxic chemical compound used in electronics manufacturing.
The company imported PCBs from Canada and then processed
them in the U.S. In the late '90s, Canada passed a law banning
the export of PCBs. (The U.S. already had a law banning their
export.) The team of attorneys at Appleton & Associates immediately identified that as a violation of NAFTA: Since S.D. Myers
was the primary company that processed that compound,
Canada's law was discriminatory, they argued.

In 1998, the tribunal—one of the first convened under
NAFTA—sided with S.D. Myers. It demanded that Canada pay
the American company $5.6 million in compensation, in addi-
tion to picking up most of its legal costs. It was huge victory
for the team at Appleton & Associates, and Appleton himself
later crowed about the power of NAFTA's investment chapter
to protect corporations' interests from unfair regulations. He
explained that the S.D. Myers case had nothing to do with PCBs
or toxic compounds or public safety, and everything to do with
whether a government had passed a law that resulted in a foreign company's lost profits. "It wouldn't matter if a substance

was liquid plutonium destined for a child's breakfast cereal," Appleton said at the time. "If the government bans a product and a U.S.-based company loses profits, the company can claim damages."

By the early 2000s, the lawyers at Appleton & Associates were no longer in a position where they had to explain what ISDS was. The cat was out of the bag. Between 2000 and 2005, a deluge of new claims poured in under NAFTA and dozens of other investment treaties worldwide. In the mid '90s, there had been about one or two new claims a year; a decade later, there were 35 every year, and counting. While corporations ended up losing more than half of all the claims they submitted under all investment treaties world wide, it was still a worthy pastime for corporate lawyers, in part because it could lead to a settlement or concession from a host government.

In one early case, for example, Appleton & Associates represented the U.S. chemical company, Ethyl Corporation, that made a gasoline additive called MMT, which the Canadian government had recently banned on the grounds that it was a potentially dangerous neurotoxin, harmful to the environment and human health. Appleton argued that the ban violated the "fair and equitable treatment" provision of NAFTA and amounted to an indirect expropriation of the company's assets. Instead of fighting the case, Canada backed down. It rescinded the regulation, paid Ethyl $13 million in compensation for the period of time that the regulation was in force, and issued a statement, on government letterhead, saying that there was no evidence that MMT was harmful. In the years since that case, every state in the U.S. has banned the chemical; it's still legal in Canada.

In another 2004 case, a group of Italian investors challenged a South African law, passed in the wake of apartheid, requiring that mining companies be at least 26 percent owned by black citizens. The law was designed to encourage racial economic equality, but the Italians claimed it amounted to an indirect expropriation of their assets and demanded $350 million in compensation under the Italy-South Africa BIT. Rather than fight the claim—and risk having to pay anywhere close to $350 million—the government backed down and waived the new law's requirements for the Italians, who publicly bragged about their legal victory.

In other cases, even when a company outright lost a claim and walked away with neither a settlement nor compensation, their lawyers would sometimes consider it victory if they succeeded in pushing the envelope on how ISDS could be used, or how the treaty language would likely be interpreted in the future. In one case in 2003, for example, a Spanish industrial waste company, Técnicas Medioambientales Tecmed, brought a claim against Mexico after the government refused to renew its license to operate a waste facility. Tecmed argued that Mexico's decision was discriminatory and amounted to an indirect expropriation of the company's assets. Mexico responded by explaining that Tecmed's original license had only been for a set period of time, and there was no contractual agreement that it would be renewed.

Mexico lost the stand-off. In 2003, the tribunal sided with Tecmed, and announced that Mexico's decision not to renew the license violated NAFTA because it frustrated Tecmed's "legitimate expectations" that the license would be renewed. The arbitrators explained:

foreign investors expect the host State to act in a consistent manner, free from ambiguity and totally transparently in its relations with the foreign investor, so that it may know beforehand any and all rules and regulations that will govern its investments, as well as the goals of the relevant policies and administrative practices or directives, to be able to plan its investment and comply with such regulations.

The Tecmed tribunal's decision echoed that of the Metalclad case. It too seemed to offer such a broad interpretation of the investment protections under NAFTA that it opened up limitless avenues for future claims. If a foreign corporation "must know beforehand any and all rules and regulations" on the books, then is its host government obligated to freeze in place its regulatory structure from the moment a corporation first invests on its soil? If a corporation invests in a foreign country expecting to be taxed at a certain rate, is its host government bound never to raise its taxes?

Give an Inch, Take a Mile

The underlying structure of ISDS also had the effect of encouraging corporations to experiment with new and creative ISDS claims. For one, making a claim was, and remains, relatively inexpensive. A 2015 study found it costs on average about $4 million to bring a claim—not exactly chump change, but hardly an insurmountable sum for a major multinational corporation.

For another, from a corporate perspective, there's very little downside. A corporation can't "lose" an ISDS claim in the same

70   way a government can. Tribunals can't force corporations to pay damages to their host state. The worst that can happen is that a tribunal can force a company to cover its host state's legal fees. But, of course, the potential upside for a corporation is huge. Merely by filing a case, a corporation can push the envelope on how investment treaty language is interpreted, or what the jurisdiction of ISDS tribunals should be. If a corporation outright wins a case, it stands to receive millions or even billions of dollars in compensation. There is no cap on how much an arbitral tribunal can award.

Those factors were exacerbated by the rules of ISDS and international investment law, which were—and remain—very loosey-goosey. The truth is, no one really knows how the language of an investment treaty or chapter will be interpreted. No one really knows how ISDS claims will be decided. By their very nature, arbitrations are subjective: Three private citizens review the language in a treaty, the details of a claim, and then decide what they think is right. Neither investors nor their host countries have any real way of really knowing for sure what those arbitrators will decide. In the early 2000s, Jacques Werner, a leading arbitration expert who has since served on more than 100 international arbitrations, worried that this dynamic threatened to make ISDS into an "arbitral casino." If there is very little to keep investors, uncertain of how a tribunal will interpret a treaty, why wouldn't they roll the dice? Maybe this time they'll win the jackpot.

In 2003, for example, two ISDS claims were filed simultaneously against the Czech Republic under the Netherlands-Czech Republic BIT. The first was brought by the company's owner,

Ronald Lauder, of Estée Lauder fame, and the second by the Netherlands-based company itself, CME Czech Republic. The circumstances that gave rise to the two claims were identical; the only difference was who had brought them. Yet, the two tribunals' decisions could not have been more different. In the first instance, the tribunal dismissed the claim out of hand. In the second, the tribunal found the Czech Republic had grossly breached its treaty obligations, and demanded that the country pay the company $353 million in damages—a sum greater than the entire annual budget for the Czech Ministry of Health. Adjusted for population size and gross national income, the size of that award in the Czech Republic was equivalent to a $131 billion award in the U.S. That's almost five times more than the U.S. government spent on Obamacare subsidies in 2015.

The two Lauder cases sent chills down government lawyers' spines. The fact that two identical claims had resulted in such dramatically different tribunal decisions underscored the uniqueness of ISDS as a subjective, supranational judicial system. Why were governments allowing these tribunals, manned by private citizens relying on vague treaty language, to essentially review their regulatory decisions? And, perhaps more to the point, why should the property claims of foreign investors trump a sovereign nation's decision to pass laws or regulate in the public interest?

Everyone agreed that foreign investors' property rights were important—but had efforts to protect them at all costs gone too far?

Property Rights

In the 1970s, University of Chicago law professor Richard Epstein proposed the now famous doctrine of "regulatory takings." In the same way that the government is obligated to compensate landowners for seizing private property to build a road or telephone line, Epstein argues that the government must also compensate owners for laws, regulations, court decisions, or other policies that diminish the value of any private property, now or in the future. In Epstein's view, his position is grounded in the Fifth Amendment: "private property [shall not] be taken for public use without just compensation." To him, the constitutional requirement to protect private property is paramount. No caveats. No exceptions.

For decades, the doctrine of regulatory takings has been the bedrock principle of the conservative movement. In the early 1980s, President Reagan's attorney general, Edwin Meese, sent a

warning to federal agencies, instructing civil servants to search
for Epstein's "hidden takings" lurking in regulations, and many
members of George H. W. Bush's cabinet later espoused their commitment to the idea. Over the last 25 years, powerful conservative
institutions in Washington, including the Federalist Society and
the Heritage Foundation, have pushed to include mentions of
"takings" in model legislation and supported the appointment of
judges in state and federal courts that back the idea.

The U.S. Supreme Court has had a more complicated
relationship with the doctrine. While many justices evince
sympathy for Epstein's ideas, they have consistently shied away
from embracing regulatory takings in its entirety. To do so, they
worry, would place the protection of private property above all
other social, political, or cultural priorities. And if they began
requiring that the government pay compensation for pretty
much every conceivable action that resulted in a partial loss of
private property—from enforcing court orders and zoning rules
to levying taxes or passing new food safety laws—they would
risk bankrupting the state. In fact if the government really were
held accountable for compensating private citizens for any *partial* loss of any private asset as a result of any government action
the regulatory state would likely cease to exist.

In an effort to balance the sanctity of property rights with
the government's need to pass laws, levy taxes, and regulate in
the public interest, the Supreme Court has drawn a line in the
sand. While the government has an obligation to compensate an
owner for the seizure or total destruction of physical property,
the justices have decided that it does not have an obligation to
compensate them for a partial diminishment of an asset. If the

74   state wants to build a highway through your backyard, it's got to
pay up. If it restricts you from using your backyard as an outdoor
concert space, it does not have to pay anything—even if its action
has a measurably negative economic impact on the value of your
land. Epstein was consistently frustrated by what he saw as the
Supreme Court's logical impurity on this front. He saw no difference between a law that directly seizes someone's property and
a law that indirectly seizes parts of it, by diminishing its value.

In the late 1990s, Epstein was in for a pleasant surprise. The
doctrine of regulatory takings, long marginalized by U.S. courts,
appeared to be quietly making inroads in supranational tribunals convened under NAFTA and other BITs. Dozens of tribunal
decisions appeared to reflect precisely Epstein's thinking, by
ordering governments to compensate companies for laws and
regulations that resulted in partial losses to the investors' and
companies' assets. "I am aware that what I have said has been
very influential in the NAFTA debate," Epstein told the journalist William Greider in 2001. "[S]trangely enough, much of what
I say seems to have more resonance in the international context
than it did in the domestic context."

The Horse Has Left the Barn

In the early 2000s, government officials began to awaken to
this new reality—and to quietly push back. Lawyers representing all three NAFTA countries began regularly attending ISDS
hearings and pressing arbitrators to use the so-called Neer Test,
which set a high bar for when a government action constituted
a violation of investor protections under the treaty. In order to

constitute a violation under that standard, a government action must rise to the level of "an outrage, to bad faith, to willful neglect of duty, or to an insufficiency of governmental action so far short of international standards that every reasonable and impartial man would readily recognize its insufficiency."

In 2001, representatives from the NAFTA countries got together to clarify the scope of the investment chapter. The idea, in part, was to carve out a clear "policy space," where governments could pass legislation and regulations in the public interest without being accused of infringing upon foreign investors' property rights. But it was tough going. U.S. and Canadian lawyers were under pressure from powerful corporations and the international business lobby to give tribunals leeway to interpret investment protections broadly. Anything that limited that scope could be used against American investors, the lobbyists argued. If the government bureaucrats constrained the language to exclude, say, a government's right to raise taxes, how would an American corporation be able to get justice if Mexico jacked up its taxes by 100 percent overnight in an effort to push it out of town? As a result, the government lawyers' effort was tepid. The resulting memorandum did not bind arbitrators from interpreting the treaty broadly, nor did it provide a robust carve-out for government regulation.

Corporate lawyers still weren't happy. They saw the government lawyers' revisions as an illegal, retroactive attempt to reinterpret the treaty text—and therefore renege on prior promises. Geoff Cowper, the private lawyer who represented Metalclad in its annulment proceeding in Vancouver, argued that the Americans and Canadians were just getting cold feet.

76 The uptick in NAFTA claims was not an indication that the language in the treaty was wrong or overly broad, he argued; it was an indication that Canadian and American government officials had had a false confidence in their own countries' respect for property rights. "I think there was a general perception by the government lawyers that their governments would not be called to account for the provisions that they had made," he told me, and when they were, it made them uncomfortable. "They did not comprehend how their own governments had been acting with impunity up until that point," he added. "There's a very compelling case that government lawyers have been trying to close the barn doors long after the horse has left."

Meanwhile, corporate lobbyists were quietly pushing to broaden the language of investment protections in future agreements. In the early 2000s, the George W. Bush administration began negotiating the Free Trade Area of the Americas, an ambitious pact that would have expanded NAFTA to include 31 additional nations. By that time, Daniel Price, who had been principal deputy general counselor of the U.S. Trade Representative from 1989 to 1992 and who is credited with crafting NAFTA's investment chapter, was representing an international business lobby that included heavy-hitter clients like GM, Dow, 3M and Chevron. He wrote to Robert Zoellick, the U.S. Trade Representative under Bush, and asked him to include language in the FTAA's investment chapter that provided corporations with "protection from regulations that diminish the value of investors' assets." Several individual NAFTA tribunals, including Metalclad's, had already interpreted the treaty in that way, but Price, acting on behalf of his clients, wanted to make sure it was set in stone.

The FTAA ended up fizzling out, but before it did, journal-   77
ist Bill Moyers asked Zoellick's right-hand man, Charles "Chip"
Roh, about Price's request in that letter. Moyers read aloud
what Price had written to Zoellick; Roh smiled uncomfort-
ably. Eventually, Roh offered an explanation. "If you took that
wording literally and said, 'OK, let's make it clear, or let's add a
rule that says, " 'By the way, expropriation means anything that
diminishes the value of your investment,' "then it seems to me...
that's a huge mistake," Roh said. "If you try to push it to there,
the people are not going to go with you. It's just too greedy."

By the mid-2000s, an international revolt against ISDS was
beginning to brew. The number of critical articles in law journals spiked, political backlash emerged, and major universities
began hosting conferences questioning the supposed "legitimacy" of a system that allowed private arbitrators to review
sovereign nations' laws. As early as 2003, the lawyer and longtime practitioner of international law Charles H. Brower II
foretold a mutiny. "The promiscuous use of [ISDS] to challenge
public regulatory laws in Canada and the U.S. has thrust it into
the center of a highly politicized debate," he wrote in a law review
article. He suggested that that polarization could not last.

At the top of critics' lists of complaints was the structure of
ISDS, which, they worried, was inherently biased against states.
A private investor can bring an ISDS claim against a sovereign
nation, but a nation can't bring an ISDS claim against an investor in return. There are no reciprocal obligations in BITs or the
investment chapters of larger trade agreements. There is no quid
pro quo. If a foreign corporation fails to pay its taxes or destroys

78   a local ecosystem, a host government has no special recourse before a private, supranational tribunal to demand compensation from a corporation. But once a government finds itself the target of an ISDS claim, that's no longer the case. The cards are stacked against it. At the very least, it must shell out money to defend itself. On average, countries spend $4.6 million dollars to defend themselves against ISDS claims, according to a 2014 Allen & Overy study. It must also weather a blow to its reputation on the international stage. "If a country is hit with an ISDS suit, it looks like it's not complying with international law," said Wellhausen, the Texas professor. "Even if the case is then dismissed or decided on behalf of the state, studies show that it's hard to shake that perception."

And then there's the specter of an ISDS tribunal actually deciding against the state—and awarding a hefty compensation package worth millions or billions of taxpayer dollars. The odds are not in countries' favor: Of all the ISDS claims that were determined to be within tribunals' jurisdictions, 61 percent were either decided in favor of investors, or states elected to settle the case, according to a 2015 ICSID report. (In general, corporate lawyers consider settlements a victory, as they often provide either compensation or a government agreement to rescind whatever law or regulation brought about the case to begin with. See Chapter 4.)

Gus Van Harten, a professor at York University's Osgoode Hall Law School in Ontario, says this dynamic creates a potentially powerful chilling effect on governments. "It's pretty clear it's an influence on the decision-making process," he said. "There's definitely a tendency to err on the side of caution," or to simply back down the moment a claim is filed, he added. As part of Van Harten's research, he and colleagues interviewed dozens of government officials in Canada about factors that contribute to how regulations are written, and which are fast-tracked. It's famously hard to gauge the real impact of a chilling effect, he cautioned, as it requires that one measure the depth of inaction. But he and other experts suggest that it's most evident in small, impoverished countries that don't have the clout or resources to go toe-to-toe with a large multinational corporation. Given an option between *not* passing a controversial law or spending millions of dollars on litigation, and opening themselves up to the possibility of having to pay a large award, most small countries will choose to simply skip the controversy entirely. Why not just repeal that offending regulation instead of going to war with a Goliath?

In 2010, for example, the international tobacco giant Philip Morris brought an ISDS claim against Uruguay on the grounds that the country's new anti-smoking law violated the U.S.-Uruguay BIT. The law limited the number of options for cigarettes that could be offered in stores. A few months after the claim was filed, Uruguay's newly elected president, José Mujica, blanched at the prospect of paying "contract lawyers at $1,500 an hour for several years" in order to fight the case. He suggested that perhaps his administration could just do a little "legal tidying up" instead. Only after a public outcry did the Bill & Melinda Gates Foundation and former mayor of New York Michael Bloomberg step in to shore up the country's legal defense fund so the case could go forward. The case is pending.

Xavier Carim, a former deputy director-general in South Africa's Department of Trade and Industry, says part of the problem is the uncertainty in how a claim will be decided—the same "arbitral casino" problem that lawyers pointed out in the early 2000s. "What was concerning for us was that you could have an international arbitration—three individuals, making a decision—on what was in effect a legislative program in South Africa that had been arrived at democratically, and that somehow this arbitration panel could potentially call this into question," he told the *Guardian*. "It was very, very clear that these treaties are open to such wide interpretations by panels, or by investors looking to challenge any government measure, with the possibility of a significant payout at the end of the day."

Private and For Profit

Under most ISDS arbitration rules, the investor or corporation that brings a claim appoints one arbitrator. The respondent country then appoints the second. The third, and last, is appointed by agreement of the other two. If the other two can't agree, a third party, such as the president of the World Bank, steps in to appoint the last member. The three arbitrators are not beholden to anyone except themselves and the people who appointed them. They represent no nation, are accountable to no democratic body, and serve as arbitrators only temporarily, drawing between $375 and $700 dollars an hour, while keeping their day jobs. Most arbitrators work as professors, corporate lawyers, or consultants to corporate boards, where they advise on ISDS-related issues.

This setup has given rise to a host of sticky conflict-of-interest concerns. Todd Tucker, a former Gates scholar at Cambridge

University, who has studied the role of arbitrators in ISDS, points out that, as a general rule, untenured arbitrators have an interest in corporations filing more claims more often: The more claims there are, the more work there is for them. "I've heard of cases where an arbitrator chairman dragged out proceedings long after it was obvious to all players that the investor's case should have been thrown out," he said. "While this could be because they're indecisive or they like the intellectual challenge of the work, it's hard to imagine the added paydays aren't a partial motivation." This dynamic is particularly true for arbitrators at the beginning and middle of their careers, he added. Unlike top arbitrators, for whom there is a constant, unceasing demand, less elite arbitrators only have work when corporations are filing dozens of cases every few months.

It's also possible, Tucker went on, for an arbitrator to switch roles within the ISDS ecosystem. In one case, an arbitrator might act as counsel to a client, arguing for a certain interpretation of a BIT or investment treaty provision, only to find himself, a few weeks later, acting as a supposedly impartial "judge," bloodlessly interpreting that same treaty provision for another case. "Does that arbitrator have an incentive to push for as expansive a definition of investor rights as possible? Potentially," Tucker said. "Add to that the fact that many arbitrators already believe in a pretty limited role for states in markets, and it's not surprising that you get some awards that seem to almost invite more filing of cases."

Many people, even critics of ISDS, are careful to underscore that the problem is not that arbitrators are rotten apples, or morally bankrupt personally. It's the *system itself* that suggests a baked-in conflict of interest: It rewards its judges financially

82 for deciding in a certain way. And unlike under most judicial systems, there are only weak rules governing when an arbitrator must recuse himself due to a conflict of interest. Under ICSID rules, for example, two arbitrators on a tribunal, or the president of the World Bank, must vote to remove a third arbitrator whose interests are in question. That almost never happens, in part because arbitrators are a close-knit crowd, and no one wants to vote a colleague off the island—especially if it means robbing her of hundreds of thousands of dollars in pay.

At the very least, the perception of impropriety has certainly become problematic. In one 2007 case, for example, a French company, Vivendi, brought a claim against Argentina over its water privatization contract. After the tribunal issued a decision in favor of Vivendi, awarding the company over $105 million in compensation, Argentina discovered that one of the arbitrators had served on the board of directors of a bank that, at the time, was the single largest shareholder in Vivendi. That arbitrator stood to gain directly from the award, and yet she did not disclose the conflict, nor recuse herself. Despite Argentina's request for an annulment, the decision stood.

Another problem is also looming. The explosion of ISDS claims in the last 15 years has meant that a very small group of arbitrators with virtually no previous experience with ISDS has been suddenly responsible for interpreting a great number of treaties all at once. According to a 2012 study by an anti-ISDS group, Corporate Europe Observatory, the same 15 lawyers have been involved in 55 percent of all ISDS claims worldwide. On the one hand, that can be seen as a good thing. That small cadre of lawyers is arguably much more experienced and efficient than any group of newcomers. But on the other hand, those private citizens, most of whom were regularly appointed by corporations, were also in a position of extraordinary power. They were not only arbitrating individual cases; they were in fact responsible for creating and fine-tuning a body of de facto precedent governing international investment law. This tiny group of private citizens, unelected and unaccountable to any democratic body has been overwhelmingly responsible for creating public international law with respect to investors.

It wasn't supposed to work that way. Investment treaties were supposed to be standalone documents, applying only to their signatory countries. In case of a dispute, each ISDS tribunal was supposed to review the particular case before it, in light of the language in the singular treaty at hand. There was no binding precedent. But that's not what actually happened. Because of the similarity of treaty language, and because the same few dozen arbitrators have served on the vast majority of tribunals, decisions have begun to reference one another, formally or informally. The way that one (theoretically independent) tribunal interprets a word or phrase in one treaty now has a profound influence on the way that another (theoretically independent) tribunal interprets that same word or phrase, found verbatim in a different treaty. If one tribunal offers a definition of, say, "expropriation" or "fair and equitable treatment," then another tribunal might reference that same definition, even though they draw from different treaties, written and ratified in different contexts.

On one level, that also can be seen as a good thing. It means that a common international investment law is emerging and

84   that the 40 or 50 international lawyers who spend most of their time working as arbitrators are aware of the same past cases, the same tribunals' interpretations. That lends coherence to the entire system and reduces the possibility that two tribunals will come out with totally conflicting decisions, as they did with those two Czech Republic cases in 2003. But on another level, is this really the way we should go about creating a global set of rules governing investment? Do we really want a few dozen private lawyers, most of whom have been repeatedly appointed by corporations, presumably because they are sympathetic to corporate interests, determining the contours of international investment law? Instead of nations' highest diplomats coming together and painstakingly hashing out the language and meaning of a multilateral investment treaty, do we want *private* lawyers doing the dirty work—essentially dictating international law with regard to investment protections?

This process has happened extraordinarily quickly. After all, for the first three decades that ISDS was on the books, private arbitrators serving on the occasional ISDS tribunal really did offer a basic dispute settlement service. Because there were so few cases, they had no choice but to act in isolation. That's changed only in the last 18 years or so. With hundreds of new ISDS claims now streaming in every few years, arbitrators today have the very real power to create a de facto set of "complementary and mutually reinforcing laws," as the legal scholar Jeswald Salacuse puts it, laying the groundwork for how sovereign governments must treat investors. That, Salacuse adds, is a very big deal indeed. That set of laws is one of the single most profound influences on modern international customary law today.

Boxing Ghosts

Osvaldo Guglielmino, the attorney general of Argentina, wasn't naive. By 2008 he was well aware of other ISDS tribunals' decisions around the world. He'd read about the controversies, witnessed the backlash, watched as activists, frustrated and outraged, decried ISDS as an impossibly biased tool. Still, he was convinced that, with the soon-to-be four dozen cases facing Argentina, he and his team would come out on top.

In the wake of the most severe financial crisis in the nation's history in 2001 and 2002, he firmly believed that Argentina had behaved well within its rights as a sovereign nation. Democratically elected lawmakers had made tough decisions during a time of profound political tumult. Those decisions had been driven by a desire to safeguard the security of the state and the safety and well-being of the Argentine people, he argued. It was unfortunate that foreign corporations and shareholders had suffered losses, but that had not been the intention of the

86   Argentine people or their representative government, he added, and they should not be punished for it.

In constructing a defense for his nation, Guglielmino leaned on two powerful trump cards embedded in both international law and investment treaties. The first was what's known as the necessity clause, a much-debated paragraph in customary international law that says a country must always abide by its treaty obligations *unless* it finds itself in severe circumstances in which it must act "to safeguard an essential interest against a grave and imminent peril."

The second was the essential security clause, which was nestled in the U.S.-Argentina BIT and hundreds of other investment treaties. It works in a similar way. It says that a nation must abide by its treaty obligations *unless* there is a severe crisis, in which case the government may take "any measures necessary for the maintenance of public order, the fulfillment of its obligations with respect to the maintenance or restoration of international peace or security, or the protection of its own essential security interests."

Guglielmino expected decisions from the four claims brought by the American gas utility companies—CMS, Enron, Sempra, and LG&E—to come down the pike first. Filed years before, all four cases had been remarkably similar. The rulings would likely foreshadow the way that other tribunals would decide the remaining three dozen cases. He and his team were confident that those decisions would strike the right note.

They shouldn't have been so optimistic. The tribunals in CMS, Enron, Sempra, and LG&E, all of which issued their decisions between 2005 and 2007, delivered almost uniformly bad news to Buenos Aires. Each found that Argentina's actions in the wake of the financial crisis had violated its obligations under the U.S.-Argentina BIT. All together, they demanded that Argentina pay roughly $200 million in compensation to the American companies—a staggering sum for a country that was already billions underwater.

From Guglielmino's perspective, that all four tribunals had decided against Argentina wasn't as bad as the fact that each tribunal had arrived at its decision on different, and often contradictory, legal grounds. There appeared to be no rhyme or reason for how the language in the U.S.-Argentina BIT was supposed to be interpreted. It seemed utterly, painfully subjective. How could he and his team move forward from there? How were they supposed to defend Argentina against dozens more ISDS claims when it appeared that treaty language regarding investor protections could be interpreted in any way the arbitrators wanted? "It was like being in a cartoon," Guglielmino said. "You are chasing and chasing, and when you have the enemy backed up against a wall, he turns around, paints a doorway onto the wall, and—pffft—he walks through it. He's gone." It was like getting into a boxing match with a ghost.

The CMS, Enron, and Sempra tribunals all found Argentina liable for violating the investment chapter of the US-Argentina BIT. But all three arrived at that conclusion on different grounds. One decided that Argentina could have been excused from its treaty obligations during a crisis, but that a *financial* crisis, however severe, couldn't count as a crisis. Another determined that a financial crisis could indeed count as a crisis, but

88   that Argentina's wasn't severe enough to qualify. (Apparently, when the country cycled through five presidents in three weeks, the police stopped showing up for work, and three dozen people were killed in street violence, the situation wasn't sufficiently "out of control," as the CMS tribunal agreed; it hadn't "become unmanageable.") A third tribunal agreed that a financial crisis could count as a crisis, and added that Argentina's was indeed severe enough to count as such, but in this case it didn't, because the Argentine government had been partially responsible for creating the crisis in the first place.

The contradictions didn't stop there. The Sempra and CMS tribunals agreed that even if the survival of the Argentine state had indeed been imperiled, the Argentine lawmakers' decisions might still have constituted a treaty violation, since they had not pursued policies that were the least restrictive to foreign investors. (The CMS tribunal even offered the government some retroactive options: Why had President Duhalde's administration not considered the "dollarization of the economy"? While "granting of subsidies to affected population," why had it not tried harder in the "restructuring of its debt"?) The CMS and Enron tribunals concluded by declaring that a country's *intentions* were essentially meaningless. It didn't matter if Argentine lawmakers had been guided by "the best of intentions, which the Tribunal has no reason to doubt," they wrote. The raison d'être of an investment treaty was to guarantee a stable framework for investment. If a country fails to do that, as Argentina had, it has breached the treaty and is liable to pay compensation.

The decision seemed to blow a giant, truck-sized hole in Guglielmino's defense—and, indeed, in any notion that a country could temporarily suspend its treaty obligations during periods of extreme crisis. Could a nation ever act quickly and defensively during a crisis? If neither the necessity clause nor the essential security clause applied in this case—at least in the eyes of three out of four tribunals—when would they? Scholars in the U.S. began to wring their hands. It was 2008 and the financial crisis was in full swing. Should the U.S. brace itself for an onslaught of ISDS claims arising out of, say, its decision to bail out the auto industry or prop up failing American banks?

The fourth tribunal, LG&E, offered the most sympathetic interpretation. Unlike the other three tribunals in the gas company cases, it decided that Argentina's financial crisis was indeed a crisis, and should count as a crisis under international law. Unlike the other three, it also determined that the Argentine government's "economic recovery package was the only means to respond to the crisis." The state's emergency measures and the subsequent political reforms came of a "desire to slow down by all the means available the severity of the crisis," the arbitrators wrote. The LG&E tribunal then went on to validate Guglielmino's defense: Argentina had indeed acted out of necessity to protect its own interests and therefore could not be held accountable for the effects of its emergency measures. "Damages suffered during the state of necessity should be born by the investor," the LG&E tribunal wrote.

The only thing that the LG&E tribunal held the Argentine government responsible for was not returning to its contractual agreements once the economy improved. When the new president, Néstor Kirchner, was elected and rose to power after April 2003, the country was no longer in a state of emergency, they decided, and should have renegotiated the gas utilities' contracts immediately, despite public protests.

While the LG&E tribunal's decision offered a bright spot in the malaise, Guglielmino and his team mostly felt trapped in a strange, alternate legal universe, where the normal rules did not apply, where the entire system hinged on the subjective interpretations of a handful of men. Surely, they thought, there would be some international body—some ultimate arbiter of justice—who would step in and say who was right?

A Very Soft Tool

There is no way to appeal an ISDS judgment but, depending on which set of arbitration rules a given tribunal has used, there are a couple options to seek redress. The first is to do what Mexico did after the Metalclad tribunal's decision: challenge a tribunal's ruling in the court of the country where the tribunal physically took place. If either party chooses that option, it must be able to claim that the tribunal's actions—or the mere existence of the tribunal itself—violated that nation's laws. If a tribunal convened in Washington, D.C., for example, then a country could file a case in the U.S. federal court system on the grounds that the arbitration should not have taken place under the bounds of U.S. law. This is a tricky path. Most countries, including the U.S., give strong deference to arbitral decisions and judges are loath to second guess arbitrators except in extreme circumstances.

The second option for redress, which is only available if the original ISDS arbitration was heard under ICSID rules, allows either the investor or the host country to assemble a three-person annulment committee. Despite the name, annulment committees have very limited jurisdiction to annul anything at all. They're not like an appellate court. They have no power to review a tribunal's legal reasoning. They cannot revisit the evidence presented in a hearing. Even if an annulment committee finds inaccuracies in how a law was interpreted, or believes the arbitrators' logic was fatally flawed, its hands are tied.

Still, that's the route that Guglielmino chose in an effort to "appeal" the CMS award. Because of the stature of the case, the annulment committee attracted some bigwigs of international investment law: Gilbert Guillaume, former president of the International Court of Justice; Nabil Elaraby, former president of the United Nations Security Council; and Australian diplomat James Crawford. After months, the three men returned with an astonishing decision. The original CMS tribunal had fundamentally misunderstood and misinterpreted international law, they decided. The tribunal had not only "made a manifest error of law," they wrote, it had applied the law "cryptically and defectively."

The decision was damning. But due to the rules of annulment committees, it was not enough to reverse the original tribunal's decision. It was not even enough to trigger a second round of arbitration. "[I]f the Committee was acting as a court of appeal, it would have to reconsider the Award on this ground," the annulment committee wrote. But since it did not have that power, it could do nothing. The tribunal vacated a small part of

92   the award that it did have jurisdiction over, and then let the rest stand.

And that was that. There was no further recourse. It was the end of the line. According to the 1958 New York Convention on the Recognition and Enforcement of Foreign Arbitral Awards, Argentina was bound by international law to enforce the ISDS tribunals' flawed decisions as if they were a decree by their own highest court. Guglielmino remembered the experience with a kind of graceful resignation. "This law has nothing to do with the hard sciences," he told me. "There is no absolute. There is no gravity. Everything is an interpretation, a technique. It's a very soft tool. And when you deal with a soft tool, whoever has the power wins."

Breaking Up Is Hard to Do

In theory, ISDS benefits countries in three main ways. The first is that it supposedly encourages foreign direct investment. Secure in the knowledge that if anything goes wrong there is a neutral judicial remedy at hand, foreign investors are, in theory, more likely to set up companies, create jobs, and build infrastructure in unfamiliar lands. It's unclear if that's how it actually works. "Today's policy literature is filled with extravagant claims about positive spillovers from [foreign direct investment]," began a 2009 report from the Federal Reserve Bank of St. Louis, "but the evidence is sobering." Ambassador Miriam Sapiro, deputy U.S. Trade Representative from 2009 to 2014 and acting U.S. Trade Representative in 2013, was less wishy-washy: "Investors rarely,

if ever, enter a foreign market because of ISDS protections," she
wrote in 2015. Brazil, which has been one of the fastest-grow-
ing economies in the last decade due largely to foreign direct
investment, has long refused to sign any BITs that include ISDS
provisions.

The second reason ISDS is sold as a benefit for countries is
that it's supposed to encourage fragile governments to evolve
more quickly—to build stronger institutions and buttress
their rule of law. Some argue that it in fact has the opposite
effect. After all, if a foreign corporation can use ISDS to do an
end-run around a national court system, the existence of that
mechanism has the effect of sidelining and marginalizing those
systems, not building them up. "If you have companies opting-
out of domestic systems and still getting good outcomes from
international arbitrators, I don't see how that's good for the
domestic courts," said Lise Johnson, the head of investment law
and policy at the Columbia Center on Sustainable Investment.

Johnson also points out that it's more difficult to make the
case that countries like the U.S., Germany, or Japan, all of which
have very highly developed court systems, would benefit from
an investment treaty in this way. If anything, ISDS claims that
circumvent developed countries' court systems would tend to
undermine judicial institutions, rather than buttress them. In
2015, for example, two American oil companies, ExxonMobil
and Murphy Oil, filed an ISDS claim against Canada. The oil
companies argued that Canada's new law, which bumped up
the amount that offshore oil producers would be required to
contribute to scientific research and development, violated

94   NAFTA. An ISDS tribunal decided in favor of the oil companies and demanded that Canada pay $17.3 million to the companies in damages. How does that improve rule of law in Canada?

The third rationale for how ISDS supposedly benefits countries is that the provisions are reciprocal: A nation's domestic investors enjoy the same treatment abroad that foreign investors enjoy on its own soil. The idea is that ISDS enforces a universal standard of treatment for investors, regardless of their nationality, operating anywhere in the world. But even that benefit is undermined when tribunals produce conflicting, contradictory or biased rulings. After reviewing the four tribunals' decisions in the U.S. gas companies' cases, for example, Argentines hardly felt that they were being afforded "global standards" of fairness.

Argentina's reaction was to revolt. Beginning in the mid-2000s, the country began systematically refusing to pay the damages awarded by ISDS tribunals. The National Congress of Argentina also threatened to withdraw from the ICSID Convention and to torch the country's BITs. A growing cadre of protesters, led in part by human rights activist and Nobel Peace Prize winner Adolfo Pérez Esquivel, encouraged the rhetoric. It was time that Buenos Aires reasserted its national sovereignty, they argued. Horacio D. Rosatti, Guglielmino's predecessor as attorney general in the early 2000s, provided legal grounding. While Argentina could bind itself to BITs and even submit arbitration, he explained, the decisions resulting from that arbitration could not be *above* the constitution. All ISDS decisions, he told me, were subject to review in Argentine courts.

While Argentina rattled its sabers, other countries began making good on their threats. In the late 2000s, Bolivia and Ecuador both renounced the ICSID and began severing more than a dozen of their respective countries' BITs. In 2012, Venezuela followed suit, and in the years since, South Africa, Indonesia, India, and Russia have all announced plans to either terminate their investment treaties or to renegotiate them when they come due. In 2015, Italy and Russia both denounced the Energy Charter Treaty, which includes ISDS. In all these cases, governments were moved to act after public outrage associated with an ISDS award.

Meanwhile, an anti-ISDS revolution in Europe has led to a series of street protests featuring banners warning of "corporate courts," while a growing number of European lawyers and judges have drawn attention to the "harm done to the public welfare by the international investment regime," according to a recent public letter. In 2014, all of the European Parliament's committees charged with reviewing the Transatlantic Trade and Investment Partnership announced, on a bipartisan basis, that they would reject ISDS in the agreement in any form. In 2015, European Union Trade Commissioner Cecilia Malmström joined the revolt, stating that she could not support a mechanism that undermines democratic governance, threatens the ability of legislatures to regulate in the public interest, and challenges European nations' sovereignty.

Guglielmino stepped down from his role as attorney general amidst this global civil war over ISDS, and found himself straddling a chasm. With an unlikely tribe, he had conducted a

96 formidable and admirable legal defense of his country. In 2009, the Global Arbitration Review ranked the Argentine attorney general's office among the best boutique law firms in the world on investment arbitration. But it was hardly an unqualified success. By 2013, Argentina was staring at nearly half a billion dollars in unpaid ISDS awards.

A Bridge Too Far

For a man who'd spent most of his life working as an economist, Rafael Correa knew how to rile a crowd. During his successful campaign for president of Ecuador in 2006, he specialized in a particular brand of populist outrage, sweeping onstage to Twisted Sister's "We're Not Gonna Take It" while promising working-class voters "a citizens' revolution" that would claw back power from entrenched elites. Some of Correa's finely tuned talking points centered on two ISDS claims, both of which involved the U.S.-based oil company Occidental Petroleum.

Occidental's first claim entered into public consciousness in 2004, when a tribunal determined that the Ecuadoran government must pay the oil company $75 million in compensation in a dispute over taxes. The details of the case, which hinged on tax refunds related to a value-added tax, were lost on the population. What mattered, Correa reminded them, was that

98   a powerful, Houston-headquartered oil company with annual revenue twice the country's GDP had convened a supra-national tribunal that could force the Ecuadoran people, 45 percent of whom lived below the poverty line, to fork over tens of millions in damages. It was an illegitimate, imperialist, and corrupt system, Correa declared, and those who defended it were "treasonous." Labor unions, human rights activists, and civil society groups rallied behind Correa's excoriations, and staged protests at Occidental's outposts in the impoverished, oil-producing Amazon provinces.

Occidental's second claim also came to light in 2004, when government officials discovered that, years earlier, the company had sold off 40 percent of its oil production rights to Alberta Energy Company without the permission of the Ecuadoran government. It was a clear breach both of Occidental's contract and of Ecuadoran law, which stated, in no uncertain terms, that transferring drilling rights without government approval would result in a terminated contract. By the time the government learned of Occidental's sale, the public was already incensed by the company's first ISDS claim, and Correa's outrage on the stump made it difficult for the government not to act.

On May 15, 2006, former minister of energy and mines Iván Rodríguez terminated the oil company's contract, then dispatched police to close Occidental's offices. The next day, the government seized the company's oil fields, including wells, drills, and storage facilities. Two days later, in the middle of a roiling presidential campaign, Occidental filed its second ISDS claim. The optics of the scene did nothing but help Correa's image as a crusader in the eyes of the people. There he was,

boldly standing up against a multinational corporation that had
grossly disrespected Ecuadoran law, facing yet another lawsuit
from some supranational tribunal in the clouds.

Correa was elected president in October 2006. Despite a career
marbled with bouts of authoritarianism and a lamentable
record on press freedom, he has remained remarkably popular
among Ecuadorans, 60 percent of whom gave him a positive job
approval rating in 2014, due in part to his unwavering commitment to the populist vision he campaigned on a decade ago.

Born into a lower middle-class family in the crowded
coastal city of Guayaquil, Correa earned grants and scholarships
to finance his education at Belgium's Université Catholique de
Louvain and the University of Illinois at Urbana-Champaign,
where he eventually earned a doctorate in economics. After
graduating, he returned to Quito, became a professor, and pursued an interest in what he saw as the structural inequities of
modern free trade agreements. Drawing in part on the work
of Korean economist Ha-Joon Chang, Correa began making
the case that modern trade agreements are inherently unfair.
By dictating how governments can govern their own domestic industrial policies, they prevent developing countries from
using the same protectionist policy tools that rich nations,
like Japan and the U.S., once used to build their own domestic industrial clout. To borrow a phrase made famous by Chang,
the wealthier nations climbed the economic rungs, then set
about "kicking away the ladder" so that developing countries
couldn't follow the same path. In the introduction to the 2006
book *The Hidden Face of Free Trade Accords*, Correa lamented

100 the "sophistry of free trade" and argued that it constricted Ecuador's development. His country, he argued, should not be stuck making "hors d'oeuvres and desserts"—a reference to the country's exports, shrimp and bananas.

Correa's career in academia was short-lived, but he carried his carefully polished perspective on trade and investment into the public sphere. After he was appointed minister of the economy in 2005, he quickly emerged as an unapologetic firebrand, willing to push for domestic spending on health and education projects over supposed fiscal necessities, like paying the country's national debt—which he dismissed as "illegitimate." When a coup created an unexpected opening in Ecuador's presidential palace, Correa was well situated to rise to the position.

In October 2012, the ISDS tribunal in the second Occidental case published its decision. The arbitrators were bitterly divided. This much they agreed on: Back in 2000, when Occidental first sold off 40 percent of its drilling rights to Alberta Energy without the government's permission, the oil company had indeed breached its contract and violated Ecuadoran law. The government's subsequent decision to terminate the company's contract was therefore lawful. Not only that, the arbitrators chided, Occidental should have expected the government's reaction.

From there, the tribunal split. Two of the three arbitrators, L. Yves Fortier and David A. R. Williams, decided that despite having behaved lawfully, Ecuador had nonetheless violated the U.S.-Ecuador BIT. The former minister's decision to seize Occidental's outposts, they determined, was "out of proportion" to the company's crime. As the majority on the tribunal, they ruled that Ecuador must pay Occidental $1.76 billion in compensation for the profits the oil company would have made, had it been able to fully exploit both its existing and not-yet-discovered oil reserves. Fortier and Williams then added another $589 million in backdated compound interest, post-award interest, and half of the costs incurred by the tribunal itself. The total award was $2.3 billion.

It was the largest ISDS award to date. As a ratio to national GDP, the award would be equivalent to requiring U.S. taxpayers to shell out $106.5 billion—more than twice as much as the U.S. spent in 2014 on housing assistance for low-income households. "To give you an idea," Pablo José Iturralde Ruiz, an activist at the Center for Economic and Social Rights in Ecuador, explained, to a reporter, "in our country the state gives a human development voucher to people who are in extreme poverty. The human development voucher means an income of $30 per family; the award is the equivalent of 15 years of human development vouchers for Ecuador's poorest families."

Brigitte Stern, the remaining arbitrator on the tribunal, was stunned by her colleagues' decision. She declared their reasoning to be "so egregious in legal terms and so full of contradictions, that I could not but express my dissent." The entire point of an investment treaty was to ensure and enforce a stable environment for foreign investors, she argued. In this case, Ecuador had been nothing if not stable: It had passed a law, signed a contract, and then abided by the terms of both. How did that constitute a punishable breach of an investment treaty?

The decision helped fuel a backlash to ISDS in Ecuador. By the time the case was decided, Correa had already renounced the

ICSID and severed the country's BITs with Cuba, the Dominican Republic, El Salvador, Guatemala, Honduras, Nicaragua, Paraguay, Romania, and Uruguay. The Ecuadoran Constitutional Court, declaring ISDS inconsistent with the country's constitution, had denounced six more BITs. To critics in Ecuador, the tribunal's decision pulled back the curtain on the system writ large. ISDS was not there to adjudicate some bloodless notion of international fairness in the treatment of investors, they argued. It was there to protect corporations' financial interests. "It's one of those cases that just seems unbelievable," said Lise Johnson of the Columbia Center on Sustainable Investment. "The decision just doesn't match the facts."

Afectados

Despite withdrawing from the ICSID and denouncing more than a dozen investment treaties, Ecuador was still in the crosshairs. Investors covered by one of the nation's remaining treaties could continue to bring ISDS claims against Ecuador using other international arbitration rules, like UNCITRAL, or forums, like the International Court of Arbitration. In 2009, the global oil company Chevron took advantage of the opening and filed a claim against Ecuador that would reverberate around the world.

Chevron's claim hinged on a trial that had spanned more than two decades and two continents, and spawned dozens of related cases, an article in *The New Yorker*, and an award-winning documentary. In Quito, the case had become something of a national touchstone. For many Ecuadorans, its byzantine twists and turns had filled headlines and nightly news spots for the entirety of their adult lives. The litigation first began in 1993, when an Ecuadoran lawyer, Cristóbal Bonifaz, filed a class action suit in a federal court in Manhattan on behalf of 30,000 rain forest residents, known as the *afectados*, or the affected ones. They were suing Chevron for failing to clean up pools of toxic oil sludge in a sliver of the Amazon known as Lago Agrio where Texaco, which had since been bought by Chevron, had operated for decades. The *afectados* claimed the toxic pools had sickened their children and animals, poisoned their water supply, and destroyed their way of life.

Bonifaz first brought the case in U.S. courts because, he explained, the Ecuadoran judiciary was notoriously corrupt and biased in favor of oil companies, which the government relied on for 30 percent of its annual budget. But Texaco's lawyers succeeded in pushing the case out of the U.S. and into Ecuadoran courts where, they claimed, the legal mores were "similar to those in many European nations." In 2003, Bonifaz re-filed the case in a courthouse in Lago Agrio, and, six years later, finally got a ruling. Judge Nicolas Zambrano, the sixth judge in Ecuador to hear the case, ruled against Chevron, awarding the *afectados* $18 billion in damages. Over a series of subsequent appeals, which eventually wended their way to the highest court in Ecuador, the award was reduced to $9.5 billion, but Zambrano's ruling stood: Chevron was on the hook.

Chevron immediately dismissed the verdict as "illegitimate and unenforceable" and filed an ISDS claim against Ecuador on

104   the grounds that the trial in Ecuador had been so corrupt, so riddled with fraud, that the final ruling was an affront to justice and amounted to a violation of the U.S.-Ecuador investment treaty. The corporation asked the ISDS tribunal either to order Ecuador to quash the $9.5 billion award or to force the country to financially compensate the company for any verdict against it. While it was waiting for the ISDS tribunal's decision, Chevron tried to get a U.S. court to issue an injunction preventing the *afectados* from collecting the award in the U.S. or anywhere else in the world, but in 2011, a U.S. federal appeals court shut the company down. U.S. courts, the judges admonished, cannot be in the business of dispensing immunity to American corporations found liable in foreign countries, even if there's evidence of fraud.

Chevron, however, had better luck with ISDS. In 2011 and 2012, the tribunal issued a series of three orders, culminating in a breathtaking directive: Ecuador must "take all measures necessary to suspend...the enforcement or recognition" of the $9.5 billion award. The *afectados'* legal right—their court judgment, enforceable under Ecuadoran law—should be enjoined, the arbitrators decided, not only in Ecuador but internationally. In January 2016, the tribunal issued its final decision, affirming its previous orders, and adding that Ecuador would be responsible for Chevron's legal expenses. The *afectados'* 23-year legal struggle appeared to have come, at last, to an abrupt end.

Correa, practically spitting the words, dismissed the decision as global "corruption" while Hewitt Pate, Chevron's vice president and general counsel, rejoiced. "The game is up," he crowed. "This award by an eminent international

tribunal confirms that the fraudulent claims against Chevron
should not have been brought in the first place."

The tribunal's decision stoked outrage and confusion both in
Ecuador and on the international stage. Even by modern international investment standards, the arbitrators' decision was
anomalous. They had decided not only to overturn a decision
made by the highest court in a sovereign land, but also to enjoin
the rights of a third party—the *afectados,* who had no legal
standing before the tribunal in the first place. Human rights
activists submitted a claim at the Inter-American Commission
on Human Rights on behalf of the *afectados* arguing that the tribunal had grossly overstepped its role. In an attempt to ensure
that a foreign investor had access to justice, they argued, it had
abrogated an entire community's access to the same.

Lise Johnson, the Columbia Center on Sustainable
Investment expert, saw the decision as a potential tipping point.
In the rapidly evolving world of ISDS, she wrote, corporations
can be expected to make "creative arguments and broad requests
for relief," but "tribunals must play the role of the reasonable
gatekeeper." Investors cannot be allowed to use broad interpretations of investment treaties "to trample through other areas
of international and domestic law, such as human rights law,"
she added. What was the proper balance between protecting the
environment and human rights and protecting the interests of
foreign investors?

At the same time, for international lawyers, activists, and
policymakers on both sides of the ISDS debate, the details of the

case raised some uncomfortable questions. After all, Chevron's underlying complaint had merit. The trial in Ecuador was unquestionably fraudulent. A series of parallel lawsuits in the U.S. had revealed reams of evidence indicating illegal actions. For example, an environmental report, supposedly authored by an "independent expert," had in fact been written by the plaintiffs' counsel, who were also accused of bribing at least one judge. And then there was the question of whether Chevron had manufactured a sting in order to discredit another judge thought to be sympathetic to the *afectados*. It was pretty clear that the proceeding failed to meet even a low standard of what constituted a fair trial.

Given that reality, many in the business community argued that it would have been grossly unfair to Chevron for the ISDS tribunal to allow the Ecuadoran court's decision to stand. Hadn't the company invested in Ecuador with the expectation that it would be treated fairly and equitably, and provided access to due process under the law, as underscored by the investor protections in the U.S.-Ecuador BIT? By allowing such a fraudulent trial to continue, Ecuador had failed to fulfill those obligations. Surely the tribunal should have the power to block the outcome of a case so problematic.

But others argued that the tribunal's decision was a bridge too far. For one, the decision revoked a legal right from the plaintiffs without providing them any representation, thus essentially asserting that Chevron's claim to justice was more substantial than the *afectados*' claim to justice. For another, Chevron had argued successfully in 2003 that the *afectados*' case should not be heard in U.S. courts, where the company almost definitely would have been afforded a fair trial. Instead, Chevron had fought to have the case heard in Ecuador. Wasn't the company now bound to that sovereign nation's judicial decision? And last, the decision appeared to set a worrisome and sweeping precedent for future cases. By signing a treaty that includes ISDS, a sovereign nation is giving private arbitrators the power to effectively annul the authoritative acts of its judiciary. The idea gave many people the willies. How would Americans react if an ISDS tribunal enjoined the verdict of a U.S. Supreme Court ruling?

The suggestion wasn't so far-fetched. In 1998, a Canadian funeral conglomerate, the Loewen Group, filed an ISDS claim against the U.S. on the grounds that a domestic court decision had been so biased that it amounted to a violation of the investment protections under NAFTA. In the underlying case, a Mississippi lawyer had used racially charged and anti-foreign language to suggest that Loewen had engaged in anti-competitive and predatory behavior. Loewen's executives were both white and Canadian. The Mississippi jury, made up of African-Americans, subsequently decided against Loewen and demanded that the company pay half a million dollars in damages to local businesses. Loewen appealed the case but it went nowhere. Having exhausted its options in the U.S. judicial system, Loewen filed an ISDS claim, demanding more than $725 million in compensation from the U.S. government. A tribunal accepted the case, thereby asserting its jurisdiction over U.S. domestic judicial decisions.

While the arbitrators ultimately decided against Loewen, the affair left a bad taste. Loewen and the American business community were incensed. By all evidence, the Mississippi case had indeed been flawed; Loewen's claim that the lawyer used racially charged language appeared to be true, and yet that did not qualify as discriminatory behavior, in breach of the investment treaty. To them, the U.S. judicial system had clearly failed. Meanwhile, U.S. government officials tugged at their collars. Too much bias to be called blameless, too many mistakes to deserve a flawless reputation, it's nevertheless true that the American judicial system is one of the most robust and reliable in the world. Why would the U.S. agree to a system that allowed three private arbitrators on a supranational panel to serve as ultimate arbiters of American justice? Theoretically, no foreign corporation should be subject to an unfair or fraudulent trial. But neither should any domestic corporation—or any natural born citizen, for that matter. If domestic corporations and American citizens must live with the imperfections of the U.S. judicial system, why shouldn't foreign corporations have to do the same?

Not Your Grandmother's Globalization

When it comes to global rules, Americans have always been conflicted. We like the idea of making them—of decreeing what is fair and what is right and what is not—and then imposing that vision of equity and prosperity on the world. We want the global rules to be *our* rules, to reflect *our* values. In 2015, President Obama pressed for the importance of the Trans-Pacific Partnership, linking the U.S. and 11 Pacific Rim nations, on precisely those grounds. "If we don't write the new rules for free trade around the world, guess what," he said ominously, "China will."

But at the same time, Americans have long been distrustful of such arrangements. After all, making global rules means that *we* have to abide by them, too. It means that, one day, those same rules could be used to constrain our actions, to force us to change course, to rein in our domestic laws or regulations, if

110   they are deemed to be in violation of some agreed-upon global standard. We love the idea of a global rulebook, but only so long as those rules allow us to do what we want.

This tension is not new. It has defined Americans' relationship with trade and investment treaties for the last 75 years. In 1944, in the bloody shadow of World War II, some of the greatest economic minds of a generation came together at a resort in Bretton Woods, New Hampshire. Four years later, they released a plan to establish the International Trade Organization, which would have created an ambitious set of global standards governing every aspect of economic cooperation. In signing it, a nation would commit to following international rules on everything from trade (tariffs, customs) to fair business practices, labors codes, and how investors would be treated on their soil. The authors of the ITO saw it not only as a multilateral trade agreement, but as a guarantor of world peace. If World War II had been the result of mercantilist competition, they reasoned, the way to guard against a reprise was not to retreat into sovereign fiefdoms, but to create regional economic dependencies, and a common, binding international law. As French Foreign Minister Robert Schuman would put it in 1950, if nations' industrial systems can be made to rely on one another, war becomes "not only unthinkable but materially impossible."

American lawmakers took one look at the ITO and scoffed. There was absolutely no way that the U.S. would bind its own sovereignty—its own ability to pass whatever laws it saw fit, to pursue whatever domestic policy it wanted— in order to adhere to some global rulebook on how things ought to be. American laws should not be forced to comply with some global standard of fairness, they decided. And that was the end of it. When

the U.S. announced it would not ratify the ITO, no one else did
either. The ITO died. American unilateral sovereignty was preserved. The nations of the world instead ratified the General
Agreement on Tariffs and Trade, a much less sweeping pact that
governed tariffs and quotas but stopped well short of dictating
what a sovereign nation's domestic policies must look like.

But between the 1940s and the 1990s, Americans had a
change of heart, motivated in part by what many in the business community saw as inequities on the global market. In the
late '70s and '80s, European and American businessmen began
complaining that nations like Japan and Korea were pursuing
domestic policies that were, in effect, unfair. They were subsi-
dizing their own agricultural and industrial goods and requiring
foreign corporations to partner with domestic firms. While
those actions didn't technically violate trade provisions under
the GATT, they still had the effect of protectionism. From those
countries' perspective, they were using their domestic policy to
nurture their industries so that they would be strong enough to
compete on the global stage. But to many in the U.S. and Europe,
it felt like cheating. Why should the Japanese government be
allowed to subsidize its domestic liquor when Jim Beam had to
compete on those same liquor store shelves?

By the mid-1980s, the administrations of Ronald Reagan
and Margaret Thatcher rose to power along with a surging, global
libertarian revolution. As the Soviet Union faltered, the nations
of the world, from East Asia to Latin America, embraced a
newfound faith in the wisdom of free markets, and set about systematically deregulating, privatizing, and shifting power away
from centralized governments and toward private investors and

112   companies. The size and strength of multinational corporations balloned and CEOs gained political clout and a sympathetic ear in Washington, D.C. Meanwhile, with tariffs, quotas, and physical barriers to free trade already at all-time lows, and with concerns over developing countries' protectionist domestic policies on the rise, the U.S. government, long skittish of compromising its sovereignty, began pushing for a binding, global rulebook governing economic fairness. That old ITO had started looking pretty good after all. It no longer felt like an imposition on U.S. sovereignty; it was sold as a boon for American economic interests—the means to squeeze more growth more quickly from the global trade regime. The libertarian revolution, combined with the prospect of rapid development in the former Soviet-controlled territories, the promise of the Internet, and the end of war, seemed bigger and more important than any stale, conscripted notion of national sovereignty.

In 1993, a U.N. Human Development Report foretold the happy end of national sovereignty as we knew it. The traditional nation-state was "too small for the big things and too big for the small things," it declared. That same year, the European Union formed, and a year later, author Kenichi Ohmae swept nationhood aside as a "nostalgic fiction." In 1994, the U.S., Canada, and Mexico signed NAFTA, and in 1995, the GATT was replaced by the World Trade Organization.

Like the ITO, its defunct predecessor, the WTO established a global rulebook on economic fairness. It governed what kind of domestic policies countries could pursue. If a nation passed a domestic law—an environmental regulation, a public health provision, an industrial policy—that broke that global rulebook,

it could be sanctioned. A tsunami of complementary trade and
investment deals quickly followed in the late '90s and early
2000s, each governing a different sector, from property rights
and services to agricultural standards. Just years earlier, those
topics had been out of bounds, the realm of sovereign nations'
hallowed domestic policy space.

Defenders of this new global paradigm rejoiced. The *New
York Times* columnist and author Thomas Friedman famously
described the WTO arrangement as a "golden straightjacket."
By choosing, voluntarily, to restrict our ability to act unilaterally—by agreeing that our laws and regulations must conform
to a global rulebook—we were committing to a greater, international ideal that promised to deliver peace, prosperity, and
riches to all the people of the earth, he wrote. Meanwhile, liberals lamented that the U.S. was giving up its sovereignty, and
worried that the WTO would restrict U.S. lawmakers' ability to
regulate corporate interests, and to legislate on behalf of con-
sumers and the environment.

That modern history leaves many Americans feeling uncertain
about the proper role of international rules, frantically toggling
between old school notions of national sovereignty—the same
impulse that led U.S. lawmakers to reject the ITO in 1948—
and the very real belief that there should be a global standard
of fairness and prosperity, so long as it's made in our image.
Americans today, on both ends of the ideological spectrum,
remain conflicted.

Conservatives, the driving political force behind the ratification of NAFTA and the WTO, are for the most part exceedingly

114   willing to bind U.S. sovereignty if it means a boon for business. In the late '90s, it was the Republican Party, backed by the Chamber of Commerce and the international business lobby, that pushed for the Multilateral Agreement on Investment, which would have established a singular, international investment treaty binding all nations to ISDS. The MAI was modeled in part on the investment chapter in NAFTA. At the same time, those same conservatives announce that it is offensive—a travesty!—that Congress might consider binding U.S. sovereignty to comply with a United Nations directive, or to participate in the International Criminal Court.

Liberals, meanwhile, live with contradictions of their own. In 1999, when the progressive left gathered to protest the WTO in Seattle, it was because they believed that that international body would constrain U.S. sovereignty, restricting lawmakers from regulating in the public interest. But their objections were also more nuanced: It wasn't that they rejected the idea of a global rulebook in any form; it was that they rejected a global rulebook that prized *economic* fairness above other priorities. Why should priority be given to the free movement of goods and services over, say, public safety? Or protecting the environment, or safeguarding the well-being of American workers?

The environmental and human rights movements today are defined not by isolationism or notions of traditional sovereignty, but, in fact, by the opposite: by the desire to bind the U.S. more tightly to multilateral agreements designed to address supranational problems, like global warming, protecting biodiversity, or eliminating human trafficking.

The modern debate over investment protections and ISDS fits into this same mold. To many, the question is not *whether* there should be global rules governing how investors and property should be treated. It is a question of who should write those rules, what those rules say, and how they should be enforced.

Take, for example, a 2015 ISDS that pitted a U.S. mining company, Bilcon, against a tiny town, Digby Neck, Nova Scotia. Bilcon wanted to build a quarry and marine terminal in an environmentally sensitive area nearby. The development would have created jobs in a region desperately in need of them. But the locals wanted nothing of it. After years of battling it out in state and local forums, a federal review board killed the project. Bilcon then filed an ISDS claim, and won: The tribunal decided among other things that Canada had frustrated Bilcon's "legitimate expectations" that it would be able to build the quarry and terminal.

The reaction to the case in the U.S. was swift—and split. The business community celebrated the decision. Governments, they argued, should be held to a strict standard to treat corporations fairly. To them, the case was clear. The Canadian government had invited Bilcon to invest in Nova Scotia, and a politically motivated environmental review board had subsequently scuttled that effort. Environmentalists and states' rights activists revolted. What was fair from Bilcon's perspective, they argued, was not fair to the people of Digby Neck. By creating a supranational judicial system, ISDS, designed to examine "fairness" through the lens of investment and investors' property, we necessarily limit ourselves to a

116   narrow view of justice. But is it possible to create a global set of investment rules—and a judicial system capable of enforcing them—that reflect some broader, Platonic ideal of "fair"?

Calibrating Sovereignty

The Obama administration says they've done it. At least as far as the TPP is concerned, U.S. Trade Representative Michael Froman says he has created an ideal set of rules governing investment protection abroad. The investment chapter of the TPP, he promises, establishes rules that are both robust and far-reaching, so as to provide the maximum protection to American corporations, while being simultaneously precise and narrow, so as to provide the maximum amount of protection to American lawmakers, working to legislate in the public interest back at home. In the face of growing alarm about the scope of ISDS, Froman has been resolute. "[N]othing we do in a trade agreement should undermine the ability of regulators on both sides to regulate in the public interest," he has said. There is nothing to worry about, he promises.

Skeptics abound. Lori Wallach, a former trade lawyer turned activist at the liberal advocacy firm Public Citizen, pointed at Article 9.15 of the TPP as an example of the TPP's flaws. To the untrained eye, it appears to do as Froman says. It appears to establish, in no uncertain terms, that foreign corporations cannot use ISDS to challenge any law or regulation written to serve the public interest. "Nothing in this Chapter," it reads, "shall be construed to prevent a Party from adopting, maintaining, or enforcing any measure otherwise consistent with this Chapter that it considers appropriate to ensure that investment activity in its territory is undertaken in a manner sensitive to environmental, health, or other regulatory objectives." "That sounds good," Wallach cautions. "But it's crap. Ask any lawyer to look at that and they'll tell you the same thing." That "otherwise consistent with this chapter" line essentially nullifies the exception, she says.

The Europeans agree. To them, the problem with ISDS is not necessarily sentiment that foreign investors should be treated fairly. It's the way those protections are interpreted, under what circumstances, and by whom. In 2015, the European Parliament announced that it would replace ISDS with a new system: the Investment Court System, which has already been included in both the European Union-Vietnam agreement and the Comprehensive Economic Trade Agreement with Canada, which was announced in February 2016. Advocates argue that the ICS reflects what's known as the "public law approach" to international investment law. By creating a court-like structure, complete with semi-permanent judges, more transparent proceedings, and an appeals mechanism based on clearly defined rules, it is supposed to more explicitly safeguard a government's right to regulate. The system also attempts to address concerns that ISDS allows corporations to do an end-run around domestic court systems by requiring that companies exhaust domestic judicial channels before turning to the ICS. It also creates reciprocal responsibilities: In return for "fair treatment," international firms commit to being "good corporate citizens," promises that are enforceable through the ICS, too.

118   Critics, meanwhile, have decried the ICS as nothing more than a "rebranding exercise," the creation of a "Zombie ISDS." Their position is more radical. To them, there's no room for investment treaties or investment chapters that create a special system to enforce investor rights at all; merely by creating a supranational court that puts corporations and governments on the same playing field, governments lose. By elevating investors' priorities to the same level as public policy, diplomats necessarily subjugate every other non-economic national priority. Why should a law designed to promote racial integration be less valuable than a law that promotes investment? Why should the suffering of 30,000 rainforest residents who have been forced to live in polluted squalor be measured against losses to Chevron's profit margin?

Many who oppose the ICS argue that investor protections simply have no place in an international treaty. Instead, they suggest, corporations themselves should be responsible for including such protections in the contracts they sign with a country. A corporation and a sovereign nation can agree on a contractual basis on whether to arbitrate at the ICSID or to adjudicate in a different nation's court system. That resulting arbitration would not constitute a *treaty* dispute, in which tribunals must rely on broad treaty language written to apply to all investors from all sectors. It would instead constitute a *contract* dispute, in which arbitrators would rely on specific contract language between one company, operating in one sector, and its host government. By making disputes about specific contracts—and not about sweeping treaty language—governments would also have the option of making reciprocal demands, advocates say.

Others push for the ultimate free market solution: If foreign corporations are worried about protecting their investments abroad, they should purchase political risk insurance on the private market. Companies like the Overseas Private Investment Corporation and the Multilateral Investment Guarantee Agency already specialize in assessing international credit worthiness or risk. If ISDS were not on the table, perhaps their business would grow to fill that void. Should a corporation decide to do business in a nation with a dicey political or legal system, then it chooses to take that risk—with, presumably, the possibility of great profit—but it has to do the cost-benefit analysis itself. Is it worth coughing up $5 million a year for a robust insurance contract, in case anything goes sideways in a nation with a long history of financial unrest?

No Exit

The backlash to ISDS has grown slowly but steadily for the last 15 years, and gained steam since the 2008 global financial crisis. In the past six years, Bolivia, Ecuador, and Venezuela have denounced the ICSID in its entirety, while at least a half dozen other nations, from Italy to South Africa to Indonesia, have vowed to renegotiate their BITs to create a more equitable balance. The question at the heart of much of this backlash is what, precisely, governments stand to gain from submitting to these supranational "courts"? To many, the negatives appear to outweigh the positives many times over (see Chapter 5).

But if these countries' roaring denunciations were intended as acts of rebellion, the reality has been somewhat meeker.

120   Even after publicly denouncing ISDS and withdrawing from the ICSID Convention, Bolivia, Ecuador, and Venezuela remain tightly bound by the strictures of international investment law. That's partly because of the complexity of how international arbitration works. ICSID is just one of several forums under which corporations can file an ISDS claim. It's also because most nations have committed to dozens of BITs and regional treaties. Denouncing four or five or ten of them still leaves them open to ISDS claims through the rest. Corporations are adept at finding inroads. By treaty shopping, they strategically base their subsidiaries in countries that have the most favorable treaty provisions with the nations where they operate.

In order to truly sever all ties to ISDS, a country would have to withdraw from the ICSID, and denounce or renegotiate *all* of its investment treaties—a move that could compromise loans from the World Bank or other international financial transactions—and even then, it would likely have to wait until the sunset clauses on those rejected treaties expired. For example, in an act of bravado in 2008, Venezuelan President Hugo Chávez unilaterally withdrew Venezuela from its BIT with the Netherlands after several global energy giants registered as Dutch corporations to take advantage of that treaty's ISDS provisions. Eight years later, the Netherlands-Venezuela BIT is still in force—and, thanks to the treaty's fine print, it will be until 2023.

Scholars and policymakers argue that the failure of developing nations to truly revolt against ISDS is evidence that, despite the frothy politics, they stand to gain from the system. Argentina, for example, spent most of the last ten years railing against the international investment regime and refused to pay ISDS awards. But it came skulking back. In 2013, it agreed to pay $450 million in outstanding arbitral awards—and three days later received a $3 billion loan from the World Bank.

To Guglielmino, the former attorney general of Argentina, the real question is not whether ISDS is good or bad. It's not whether Argentina should torch its BITs, or whether investors should have protections. Developing nations like Argentina remain in the system, he says, because they have no other responsible choice. In the modern, globalized world, isolationism is a "childish thing, an illusion—a mixture of illiteracy and searching for magical solutions," he says. The best a nation can do is to stay in it, to fight like hell, and slowly push for justice and reform from within.

At a conference in Chile in 2005, Tom Kruse, an American who was at the time advising the Bolivian government, overheard a member of Guglielmino's team describing Argentina's apparent unwillingness to leave the ICSID in terms of a cowboy standing over a cow's carcass. "He said, 'There are vultures circling overhead and they want to land and pick the carcass clean. And it's my job to stand around the carcass with a shotgun and once in a while blast off a shell so they don't land,'" Kruse said, recounting the lawyer's story. He laughed. "So I asked the lawyer why Argentina didn't leave the system, and he said, 'It wouldn't stop the vultures. I have to keep blasting off these shots or we're done.'"

University of Texas at Austin government professor Rachel Wellhausen's *The Shield of Nationality: When Governments Break Contracts with Foreign Firms* (Cambridge University Press, 2015) takes a shrewd look at when governments break their promises to foreign investors, and why. The book is based on Wellhausen's award-winning doctoral dissertation and draws in part on more than 150 interviews with investors in the former Soviet bloc.

For a short and accessible analysis of global governance, international investment, and ISDS, see former University of Cambridge Gates Scholar Todd Tucker's excellent blog, Under Two Ceilings, at toddntucker.com. Updated regularly, Tucker's blog is often the first to offer thoughtful insight when ISDS shows up in the news cycle.

Simon Lester, a trade policy analyst at the libertarian Cato Institute's Herbert A. Stiefel Center for Trade Policy Studies also keeps an accessible blog, the International Economic Law and Policy Blog, at worldtradelaw.typepad.com. Lester offers a clear-eyed, and often highly critical, take on ISDS-related news.

As a historian and an investment lawyer, Todd Weiler's *The Interpretation of International Investment Law: Equality, Discrimination and Minimum Standards of Treatment in Historical Context* (Brill, 2013) offers a unique view on ISDS. He argues that modern lawyers have an obligation to apply a historical lens to the development and interpretation of investment law.

Gus Van Harten, an international investment law professor at the Osgoode Hall Law School at York University in Toronto, rolled his PhD thesis at the London School of Economics into the first book-length primer on investor-state dispute settlement, *Investment Treaty Arbitration and Public Law* (Oxford University Press, 2007). This dense, carefully researched work of historic and legal scholarship builds to a searing condemnation of what ISDS has become today.

Andrew Newcombe, a law professor at the University of Victoria, and Lluís Paradell, counsel at one of the biggest ISDS firms in the world, Freshfields Bruckhaus Deringer, joined together to write *Law and Practice of Investment Treaties: Standards of Treatment* (Kluwer Law International, 2009). What it lacks in accessibility—it was written by lawyers for lawyers—it makes up for in practical insight into how investment disputes are litigated in real life.

The Regulation of International Trade, 4th edition (Routledge, 2012), is
an encyclopedic survey of international laws and rules. While they do
not focus on ISDS in particular, authors Michael Trebilcock, Robert
Howse, and Antonia Eliason offer invaluable context for how investment
protections fit into the larger trend of rulemaking through international
treaties.

Kenneth J. Vandevelde, who most recently served in the Obama
administration as a White House policy analyst, has spent the last 30 years
representing the U.S. as a treaty negotiator and in various other capacities
before the International Court of Justice, the Iran–United States Claims
Tribunal, and The Hague. His book *Bilateral Investment Treaties: History,
Policy, and Interpretation* (Oxford University Press, 2010) offers a unified
theory of the impact of bilateral investment treaties worldwide.

*Looking to the Future: Essays on International Law in Honor of W. Michael
Reisman* (Brill, 2011) is a hulking compendium of 52 essays, written by some
of the most eminent ISDS arbitrators, lawyers, and scholars worldwide.
While it's intended for an audience of other investment lawyers and
scholars, and therefore predictably falls a few rungs below "beach reading,"
it offers a wide-ranging, and sometimes contentious, view from the top.

In her book, *The Expropriation of Environmental Governance: Protecting
Foreign Investors at the Expense of Public Policy* (Cambridge University Press,
2009) Australian National University researcher Kyla Tienhaara offers a
condemnation of ISDS though the lens of environmentalism.

Decorated with bright graphics and a colorful layout, Pia Eberhardt
and Cecilia Olivet's e-book *Profiting from Injustice* (Corporate Europe
Observatory and the Transnational Institute, 2012) is intended as a
piece of accessible advocacy. Eberhardt and Olivet, who are both active
in the political fight against ISDS, nevertheless offer a well-researched
condemnation of the mechanism.

*The Selling of "Free Trade": NAFTA, Washington, and the Subversion of
American Democracy* (University of California Press, 2000) was published
before ISDS was on anyone's radar, but author and president of *Harper's
Magazine* John R. MacArthur shrewdly lays the economic and philosophical
groundwork of what is to come.

Harvard professor and longtime trade expert Dani Rodrik's *The
Globalization Paradox: Democracy and the Future of the World Economy*

124   (Norton, 2011) offers probably the most concise, readable, and cogent analyses of how profoundly the world has shifted between 1994 and today.

Supreme Court Justice Steven Breyer's *The Court and the World: American Law and the New Global Realities* (Knopf, 2015) mentions investment treaties only passingly—a half dozen times, at most—and yet the book, which explores how U.S. laws should be applied in evermore global contexts, lays the intellectual foundation for post-modern, rule-based globalization. In chapter 8, which explores investment treaty arbitration, Breyer offers an invaluable analysis of how U.S. law empowers and accepts international arbitral decisions, and raises a host of troublesome questions about what comes next.

For an impressively entertaining description of how the World Trade Organization works—and doesn't—in this ever shifting global economy, see former *Washington Post* journalist Paul Blustein's *Misadventures of the Most Favored Nations: Clashing Egos, Inflated Ambitions, and the Great Shambles of the World Trade System* (PublicAffairs, 2009). Another wonderful book by Blustein, *And the Money Kept Rolling In (And Out): Wall Street, the IMF, and the Bankrupting of Argentina* (PublicAffairs, 2006), traces with journalistic verve the tumultuous aftermath of the Argentine financial collapse.

ENDNOTES

CHAPTER ONE

13 **first appeared in treaties in 1969:** "Conceptual Difficulties in the Empirical Study of Bilateral Investment Treaties," by Jason Yackee, *Brooklyn Journal of International Law*, 2008. The first bilateral investment treaty was signed between the United Kingdom and Pakistan in 1959, but the first to include full-fledged arbitral pre-consent, a precondition for ISDS, was between Italy and Chad in 1969. http://papers.ssrn.com/sol3/papers.cfm?abstract_id=1015088.

14 **must pay the company $460,000:** *Asian Agricultural Products, Ltd. v. Sri Lanka*, ICSID, award issued June 17, 1990. http://www.italaw.com/sites/default/files/case-documents/ita1034.pdf.

14 **very political indeed:** *Reshaping the Investor-State Dispute Settlement System: Journeys for the 21st Century,* edited by Jean E. Kalicki and Anna Joubin-Bret, Brill 2015.

14 **there have been 647:** Investment Policy Hub, a United Nations Conference on Trade and Development website, keeps track of most recent ISDS cases. http://investmentpolicyhub.

unctad.org/ISDS?status=1000. See also "World Investment Report 2015," UNCTAD. http://unctad.org/en/PublicationsLibrary/wir2015_en.pdf.

15 **from NAFTA and Central American Free Trade Agreement to the Energy Charter:** A list of all NAFTA claims is available at a website maintained by the private lawyer Todd Weiler. http://www.naftaclaims.com/disputes-with-usa.html. As of 2015, the Energy Charter Treaty surpassed NAFTA as the international investment agreement invoked most frequently (60 and 53 cases, respectively). "Recent Policy Developments and Key Issues, Chapter III," World Investment Report. http://unctad.org/en/PublicationChapters/wir2015ch3_en.pdf.

16 **no way to appeal an ISDS award:** The possibility of creating an ISDS appellate body comes up time and again in discussion of reforming ISDS. For a primer, see "The Legitimacy Crisis in Investment Treaty Arbitration: Privatizing Public International Law Through Inconsistent Decisions," by Susan D. Franck, Fordham Law Review, Vol. 73, 2005.

17 **increase that ratio significantly:** Exact numbers are tricky to come by since the U.S. already has bilateral investment

treaties with some countries slated to be signatories to the TPP and TTIP. Trade between the U.S. and EU accounts for about half of the global GDP. Trade between the U.S. and the 11 other TPP countries accounts for about 40 percent. "What You Need To Know About TPP," European American Chamber of Commerce. http://www.eaccny.com/international-business-resources/what-you-need-to-know-about-ttip/. "Overview of the Trans Pacific Partnership," U.S. Trade Representative. https://ustr.gov/tpp/overview-of-the-TPP.

18   **National Conference of State Legislatures:** "Free Trade and Federalism," National Conference of State Legislatures. http://www.ncsl.org/ncsl-in-dc/standing-committees/labor-and-economic-development/free-trade-and-federalism.aspx.

13   **long refused to confirm the U.S.:** "U.S. Opposition to the International Criminal Court," Global Policy Forum, 2003–2012. https://www.globalpolicy.org/us-un-and-international-law-8-24/us-opposition-to-the-icc-8-29.html.

19   **annul the authoritative acts of its legislature:** *BG Group, PLC v. Republic of Argentina*, dissent by Chief Justice John Roberts, 2014, quoting the legal scholar Jeswald Salacuse.

19   **an American oil and gas company filed an ISDS:** Lone Pine Resources Inc. v. The Government of Canada, ICSID Case No. UNCT/15/2.

20   **hyperbolic "bunk" and "totally wrong":** "Is TPP trade deal a massive giveaway to major corporations? An exchange between Obama and Sherrod Brown," by Greg Sargent, *Washington Post*, April 27, 2015.

23   **half of all of the claims:** By the end of 2015, Argentina was facing 54 claims. Concluded and pending cases before ICSID available at "International Centre for Settlement of Investment Disputes: ICSID Cases," database maintained by World Bank Group. http://www.worldbank.org/icsid/cases/cases.htm.

25   **predilection for signing investment treaties:** "Bilateral Investment Treaties 1959–1999," UNCTAD, Dec. 2000. http://www.unctad.org/en/docs/poiteiiad2.en.pdf.

27   **the convertibility law:** "The Failure of the Debt-Based Development: Lessons from Argentina," by Eugenio Bruno, *Cato Journal*, Vol 2, No. 2, Spring/Summer 2006.

27   **"stable investment climate":** For example, in many of its

128 contracts with foreign bondholders, Argentina promised to submit any future disputes to New York courts, and to waive sovereign immunity. Anyone who's been paying attention to Argentina in the last 15 years is well aware of the protracted legal drama between bondholders who agreed to renegotiate repayment with Argentina and those—"the holdouts" or "vulture funds"—who did not. Those disputes, while fascinating, played out mostly in New York courts, which had been specified as the judicial forum in contracts, not before ISDS tribunals.

27   **debt piled up:** *Argentina and the Fund: From Triumph to Tragedy*, by former IMF Chief Economist Michael Mussa, Peterson Institute 2002. Also see, *And the Money Kept Rolling In (And Out): Wall Street, the IMF, and the Bankrupting of Argentina*, by Paul Blustein, Public Affairs 2005.

30   **withered to $2,800:** "Special Report, Argentina's Collapse: A Decline Without Parallel," *The Economist*, Mar. 2, 2002.

30   **1.2 million people moved onto the streets:** "Slump Turns Jobless Argentines Into Scavengers," *Associated Press*, Sept. 22, 2002.

30   **"with its republican form of government intact":** *Investment Treaty Arbitration and Public Law* by Gus Van Harten, reference to *CMS Gas Transmission Company v. Argentina*, awarded May 12, 2005. http://www.italaw.com/cases/288.

30   **Enron:** Enron went bankrupt in 2001. Those pursuing this settlement had little or nothing to do with the corporation that was supposedly harmed, leading many critics to raise the specter of debtors and jilted shareholders acting in essence like ISDS trolls— using the mechanism as a means to salvage losses, rather than claim legitimate harm.

30   **among other things:** The companies' contracts also included a blanket promise, what's known as a "stabilization clause," binding Argentina to maintaining a stable investment environment. Any change to the investment environment would constitute a breach of contract. "Regulatory Takings, Stabilization Clauses, and Sustainable Development, by Lorenzo Cotula, Global Forum on International Investment, March 27–28, 2008, http://www.oecd.org/investment/globalforum/40311122.pdf.

CHAPTER TWO

30   **an alien in an alien land:** Scholars of this fascinating history will no doubt recoil at the omissions in this very brief summary. For a much more

thorough review of this literature, see the following works, upon which this sketch is based. *Law and Practice of Investment Treaties: Standards of Treatment*, by Andrew Newcombe and Lluís Paradell, Kluwer Law International, 2009. *The Regulation of International Trade*, 4th edition, by Michael Trebilcock, Robert Howse, and Antonia Eliason, Routledge, 2012. *The Evolution of International Trade Agreements*, by Gilbert Winham, University of Toronto Press, 1992. "The Rise of Free Trade in Western Europe, 1820–1875," by Charles P. Kindleberger, *Journal of Economic History* 1975. *Bilateral Investment Treaties: History, Policy, and Interpretation*, by Kenneth J. Vandevelde, Oxford University Press 2010. *Standing Guard: Protecting Foreign Capital in the Nineteenth and Twentieth Centuries*, by C. Lipson, University of California Press, 1985. *Looking to the Future: Essays on International Law in Honor of W. Michael Reisman*, "Chapter 33: The Once and Future Investment Regime," by Jose E. Alvarez, Brill, 2011. *The Purpose of Intervention: Changing Beliefs about the Use of Force*, by Martha Finnemore, Cornell University Press, 2003.

34   **"Whoever ill-treats a citizen indirectly injures the State":** *The Law of Nations, or the Principles of Natural Law*, by Emer de Vattel, Classics of International Law, Book II, Chapter VI at 136 (ed. C. Fenwick transl. 1916).

36   **Carlos Calvo:** *Le Droit International Theorique et Pratique*, 5th edition, by Carlos Calvo, 1868.

37   **"the purely pecuniary interests":** "'Prompt, Adequate and Effective': A Universal Standard of Compensation?," by Frank G. Dawson and Burns H. Weston, *Fordham Law Review*, 1962.

38   **Organization for Economic Cooperation and Development:** It was, at the time, the Organization for European Economic Cooperation.

38   **"the Capitalist Magna Carta":** "The Capitalist Challenge: The Capitalist Magna Carta," *Time*, Oct. 28, 1957.

39   **win-win for everyone:** In the 1950s, Hermann Josef Abs, the director of the Deutsche Bank of Frankfurt and a personal adviser to Germany's economic minister, and Lord Hartley Shawcross, a former attorney general of the U.K. proposed one of the most comprehensive multilateral investment treaties. In 1955, a delegation from the International Chamber of Commerce described the potential of the future convention as a piece of legislation that "would be a constructive step towards facilitating international trade, and ultimately towards

higher standards of living and so towards general peace and prosperity." See also, "The Abs-Shawcross Draft Convention on Investments Abroad," by Greg Schwarzenberger, *Oxford Journals*, Vol. 14, Issue 1, 1961.

39   from the Middle East to Latin America: Iran nationalized British oil assets in 1951; Libya expropriated Liamco's concessions in 1955; Egypt nationalized the Suez Canal in 1956; Cuba nationalized sugar interests in the 1960s. *Sovereignty Over Natural Resources: Balancing Rights and Duties*, by Nico Schrijver, Cambridge University, Press 1997; *Transnational Legal Problems, 4th Edition*, by Henry J. Steiner, Detlev F. Vagts, and Harold Hongju Koh Foundation Press, 1994.

39   They then dropped off: There were only 17 in the 1980s and 22 in the 1990s. A total of 24 countries accounted for all of the expropriations between 1989 and 2006. "Expropriation of Foreign Direct Investments: Sectoral Patterns from 1993 to 2006," by Christopher Hajzler, *Review of World Economics*, 2012.

40   foreign control through bureaucratic means: "Protection of Private Foreign Investment by Multilateral Convention," by Arthur S. Miller, *The American Journal of International Law*, Vol. 53, No. 2,

April 1959, citing the *New York Times*, October, 16, 1957.

40   "permanent sovereignty over natural resources": "U.N. Charter of Economic Rights and Duties of States," General Assembly Resolution, December 12, 1974, and "General Assembly Resolution 1803, XVII," Dec. 14, 1962. See also, "The Global Governance of Foreign Investment: Madly Off In All Directions," by Luke Erik Peterson, *Dialogue on Globalization*, No. 19, May 2005.

41   just one other investment partner: *Foreign Investment Disputes: Cases, Materials and Commentary,* by R. Doak Bishop, James Crawford, and W. Michael Reisman, Kluwer Law International, 2014.

41   BITs were vague: "The Emerging Global Regime for Investment" by Jeswald W. Salacuse, *Harvard International Law Journal*, Vol. 51, No. 2, Summer 2010. See also *The Law of Investment Treaties*, by Jeswald W. Salacuse, Oxford University Press, 2010. "The WTO's World Trade Report 2011: The WTO and Preferential Trade Agreements: From Co-existence to Coherence," World Trade Organization, 2011. www. wto.org/english/res e/publications e/wtf11e.htm.

41   thus binding a nation to arbitration: The *Asian Agricultural*

Products, Ltd. v. Sri Lanka award, 1990, was the first to confirm that a country in fact consented to arbitration through its previous consent to an investment treaty.

41 **prisoners' dilemma:** "Why LDCs Sign Treaties That Hurt Them: Explaining the Popularity of Bilateral Investment Treaties," Andrew T. Guzman, *Virginia Journal of International Law* 639, 1998.

41 **385 BITs:** "Treaties and Regulatory Risk in Infrastructure Investment," by Thomas Walde and Stephen Dow, *Journal of World Trade*, Vol. 34, Issue 2, 2000.

44 **more than 3,271 investment treaties:** 2,926 BITs and 345 "other IIAs"; UNCTAD 2015 report. Not all investment treaties include ISDS, although most do. http://unctad. org/en/PublicationChapters/ wir2015ch3_en.pdf.

44 **important tipping point:** President Bill Clinton signed NAFTA on December 8, 1993, and it later passed the Senate 61 to 38, with just more than half of Democrats voting against it. It passed the House 234 to 200 entirely on the strength of Republican votes. It went into effect January 1, 1995. "A brave new Lochner era? The constitutionality of NAFTA Chapter 11," by Steve Louthan, *Vanderbilt Journal of Transnational Law*, November 1, 2001.

44 **close investment partners:** U.S.–Canada trade accounts for $658 billion, U.S.–Mexico accounts for $534 billion. "Trans-Pacific Partnership Is Reached, but Faces Scrutiny in Congress," by Jackie Calmes, *New York Times*, Oct. 5, 2015.

44 **public records:** Many early investment treaties allowed ISDS claims to remain secret. As a result, scholars today only know about cases where both parties agreed to make the claim public, or where one party leaked information. Some BITs today, including the Sweden–Germany BIT, still allow tribunals to hear claims in secret.

CHAPTER THREE

46 **Metalclad Corporation:** All references, quotes, sworn testimony, and statements of facts, in this chapter refer to original Metalclad case documents, available at NAFTAClaims.com. http://naftaclaims.com/disputes-with-mexico.html.

48 **a report expressing "doubts":** "Courtesy Translation of the Witness Statement of Dr. Pedro Medellin Milan." http://nsarchive. gwu.edu/NSAEBB/NSAEBB65/ medellin.pdf.

56 **constitute an expropriation:** They also determined that the Mexican officials, by failing to make clear to Metalclad "all relevant legal

132 requirements" and to correct "any scope for misunderstanding or confusion," had violated the spirit of the treaty. It was a definition that had never before been applied to interpretations of the "minimum standard of treatment" under customary international law.

57 **any new law or regulation:** See also, "The Boundaries of Regulatory Expropriation in International Law," by Andrew Newcombe, *ICSID Review for Investment Law Journal*, Vol. 20, No. 1, 9–11, 2005.

57 **Decisions are final and binding:** According to the 1958 New York Convention on the Recognition and Enforcement of Foreign Arbitral Awards. http://www.uncitral.org/uncitral/en/uncitral_texts/arbitration/NYConvention.html.

CHAPTER FOUR

60 **Jackson's book:** *World Trade and the Law of GATT*, by John H. Jackson, Lexis Law Pub, June 1969.

62 **percentage of foreign direct investment:** "FDI In Figures October 2015," The Organisation for Economic Co-operation and Development.

62 **investment treaties began to explode:** "Tearing Down the Great Wall: The New Generation Investment Treaties of the People's Republic of China," by Stephan W. Schill, *Cardozo Journal of International and Comparative Law*, 2007.

62 **Cuba signed more than 60:** See Alvarez's "The Once and Future Foreign Investment Regime," supra note.

63 **did not bother with fine print:** The United States' Model Bilateral Investment Treaty—the one it used as a template—was six pages long and contained just a two-page article on ISDS. The 2012 U.S. Model BIT, by contrast, contains 13 articles, which cover more than 12 pages of the treaty, and include detailed provision on the elements of consent to arbitration, consolidation of claims sharing similar questions of fact and law, steps to promote the efficiency and transparency of the proceedings, determination of the governing law for disputes, and so forth. "Reform of Investor-State Dispute Settlement: The U.S. Experience," by Jeremy K. Sharpe, in *Reshaping the Investor-State Dispute Settlement System: Journeys for the 21st Century*, edited by Jean E. Kalicki and Anna Joubin-Bret, Brill 2015.

65 **14-fold increase:** Between 1996 and 2005, 166 investor claims were registered at ICSID, compared to 35 in the previous 30 years. See "ICSID Caseload Statistics,"

International Centre for Settlement of Investment Disputes.

65 **four were against the U.S., and six were against Canada:** By August 2000, four cases had proceeded to an ISDS tribunal on the merits: *Azinian v. Mexico*, Metalclad, *S.D. Myers v. Canada*, and *Pope & Talbot v. Canada*.

63 **regulate in the public interest:** "International Investment Law: Understanding Concepts and Tracking Innovations," OECD, 2008. See also, "Emergence of the International Center for Settlement of Investment Disputes as the most Significant Forum for Submission of Bilateral Investment Treaty Disputes," by William D. Rogers, presentation to Inter-American Development Bank Conference, October 26–27, 2000.

64 **the legal definition of "fair":** See, for example, "Fair and Equitable Treatment Minimum Standard of Treatment," a presentation by Nathalie Bernasconi-Osterwalder, International Institute for Sustainable Development.

64 **"I know it when I see it":** "Indirect Expropriation in the Law of International Investment: I Know It When I See It, or Caveat Investor," by L. Yves Fortier and Stephen L. Drymer, *ICSID Review*, 2004.

65 **the front lines:** In the last 20 years, there have been 80 cases under NAFTA, with 22 claims against the U.S., 24 against Mexico, and 34 against Canada. Another useful benchmark: Between 1972 and 2000, ISDS tribunals under ICSID rules handed out 31 awards total. From 2001 to 2010, it handed out 96. From 2011 to June 2015, it handed out 82. Naftaclaims.com

67 **no evidence that MMT was harmful:** "Thirteen Years of NAFTA's Chapter 11: The Criticisms, the United States' Responses, and Lessons Learned," by Catherine M. Amirfar and Elyse M. Dreyer, *New York International Law Review*, 2007.

68 **26 percent owned by a black citizens:** *Piero Foresti, Laura de Carli & Others v. The Republic of South Africa*, ICSID, award issued August 4, 2010.

68 **brought a claim against Mexico:** *Técnicas Medioambientales Tecmed, S.A. v. The United Mexican States*, ICSID Case No. ARB (AF)/00/2.

69 **freeze in place:** "At What Time Must Legitimate Expectations Exist?," by Christopher Schreuer and Ursula Kriebaum, A Liber Amicorum: Thomas Wälde, edited by Jacques Werner and Arif Hyder Ali, Cameron May, 2009. See also "Indirect Expropriation in

134 Investment Treaty Arbitrations," by
Jan Paulsson and Zachary Douglas,
*Arbitrating Foreign Investment
Disputes*, edited by Norbert
Horn & Stefan Kröll, Kluwer Law
International, 2004.

**69 how treaty language is
interpreted:** See, for example,
*Methanex Corporation v. United
States of America*, UNCITRAL,
award August 3, 2005. In 1999,
a Canadian chemical company,
Methanex, challenged a California
law phasing out a gasoline additive
that was contaminating drinking
water around the state. Methanex,
which made a chemical in that
additive, demanded $970 million
in damages. While that tribunal
ultimately decided in favor of the
U.S. government, the fact that the
challenge was deemed a legitimate
ISDS claim helped trigger the first
wave of media attention on ISDS.

70 "arbitral casino": "Making
Investment Arbitration More
Certain—a Modest Proposal," by
Jacques Werner, *Journal of World
Investment*, No. 5, 2003. See also,
"The Creeping Codification of
Transnational Commercial Law: An
Arbitrator's Perspective," by
Charles N. Brower and Jeremy K.
Sharpe, *Journal of World Investment*,
No. 2, April 2003.

70 CME Czech Republic: *Ronald
S. Lauder v. Czech Republic and CME
Czech Republic BV v. Czech Republic*.
"Power, Authority and International

Investment Law," by Tai-Heng
Cheng, *American University
International Law Review*, 2005.

**71 five times more than the U.S.
government spent on Obamacare:**
"Policy Basics: Where Do Our
Federal Tax Dollars Go?" Center on
Budget and Policy Priorities, March
2016.

**73 the regulatory state would
likely cease to exist:** "The Global
Fifth Amendment? NAFTA's
Investment Protections and
the Misguided Quest for an
International 'Regulatory Takings'
Doctrine," by Vicki L. Been and Joel
C. Beauvais, *New York University
Law Review*, Vol. 78, No. 1, 2006.

74 Neer Test: In 1926, the
U.S.–Mexico General Claims
Commission attempted to
define what it meant to provide
inadequate treatment to a foreign
investor. "The treatment of an
alien, in order to constitute an
international delinquency, should
amount to an outrage, to bad faith,
to willful neglect of duty, or to
an insufficiency of government
action so far short of international
standards that every reasonable
and impartial man would readily
recognize its insufficiency."
"Reports of International Arbitral
Awards," *Pauline Neer v. United
Mexican States, October, 15* 1926.

76 31 additional nations: The
FTAA eventually lost steam,

replaced in part by the Central American Free Trade Agreement in 2005.

76   Daniel Price: Price now serves, at Obama's behest, on the Panel of Arbitrators at ICSID.

77   articles in law journals spiked: "Revisiting History: How the Past Matters for the Present Backlash Against the Foreign Investment Regime," by Asha Kaushal, *Harvard International Law Journal*, 2005. See also, "Investment Protection in Extraordinary Times: The Interpretation and Application of Non-Precluded Measures Provisions in Bilateral Investment Treaties," by William W. Burke-White & Andreas von Staden, *Virginia Journal of International Law*, 2008. *Making Foreign Investment Safe: Property Rights and National Sovereignty*, by Louis T. Wells and Rafi Q. Ahmed, Oxford University Press, 2007. "Memorandum from Karl P. Sauvant, Executive Director, Vale Columbia Center on Sustainable International Investment, and other colleagues at Columbia University, to the Office of the President, Secretary of State, Secretary of the Treasury, Director of the National Economic Council, and U.S. Trade Representative," Jan. 29, 2009.

77   foretold a mutiny: "NAFTA's Powerful Little Secret; Obscure Tribunals Settle Disputes, But Go Too Far, Critics Say," by Anthony DePalma, *New York Times*, March 11, 2001.

77   inherently biased against states: States can file counterclaims pursuant to Rule 40 of the ICSID Arbitration Rules under certain circumstances. Such claims are rare.

77   a host government has no special recourse: This remains a major complaint against ISDS today, even from major players within the system. *The Regulation of International Trade*, 4th edition, by Michael Trebilcock, Robert Howse, Antonia Eliason, 2012. "In our view, a successful multilateral alternative will have to link investor rights to investor responsibilities, through a binding code of conduct. It must also allow space for the kind of interventionist policies that credible economic analyses suggest may have supported rapid and real economic growth and development in economies such as South Korea."

78   2014 Allen & Overy study: "How Much Does an ICSID Arbitration Cost? A Snapshot of the Last Five Years" by Jeffery P. Commission, Kluwer Arbitration Blog, February 29, 2016. The study, based on a review of 176 ISDS awards, concluded that average cost of litigation is $9 million, with governments shouldering, on average, $4,559,000.

79   Philip Morris brought an ISDS claim: "Galvanizing

136 global action towards a tobacco-free world," keynote address at the 15th World Conference on Tobacco and Health, Singapore, by Dr. Margaret Chan, Director-General of the World Health Organization, March 20, 2012: The threat of international litigation is "deliberately designed to instill fear. The wolf is no longer in sheep's clothing, and its teeth are bared." Chan pointed at the tactics of the world's biggest tobacco companies and their corporate allies, which, for decades, have sent letters, often on International Chamber of Commerce letterhead, to countries warning them that if they pass laws restricting the consumption of cigarettes, they may be in violation of treaty obligations. If such laws are found to be in violation, the letters calmly inform, then the government will be required to pay compensation. Malaysia, Togo, Namibia, New Zealand, Canada, and the United Kingdom have all received these notes. http://www.who.int/dg/speeches/2012/tobacco_20120320/en/.

79 **"What was concerning for us" he told** the *Guardian*: "The Obscure Legal System That Lets Corporations Sue Countries," by Claire Provost and Matt Kennard, the *Guardian*, June 10, 2015. See also "The New Masters of the Universe," by Frances Maguire, *Banker*, Jan. 2, 2006; "The Top 200: The Rise of Corporate Global Power," by Sarah Anderson and John Cavanagh, Institute for Policy Studies, Dec. 2000.

79 **shore up the country's legal defense fund:** "Part III: Uruguay vs. Philip Morris Tobacco giant wages legal fight over South America's toughest smoking controls" by Claudio Paolillo, Center for Public Integrity, November 15, 2010. https://www.publicintegrity.org/2010/11/15/4036/part-iii-uruguay-vs-philip-morris.

80 **more work there is for them:** Conservative thinkers argue that since corporations and governments appoint arbitrators to a panel, arbitrators are dependent on those parties alone and normal conflict-of-interest rules are less important. "Judicial Independence in International Tribunals," by Eric A. Posner and John C. Yoo, *California Law Review*, 2005. See also, "Power and Persuasion in Investment Treaty Interpretation: The Dual Role of States," by Anthea Roberts, *American Journal of International Law*, 2010.

81 **whose interests are in question:** "Regulations and Rules," ICSID, April 2006. https://icsid.worldbank.org/ICSID/StaticFiles/basicdoc/CRR_English-final.pdf.

82 **perception of impropriety:** "Same arbitrator repeatedly appointed by the same party:

a case for disqualification?" Allen & Overy, Sept. 8, 2011. http://www.allenovery.com/publications/en-gb/Pages/Same-arbitrator-repeatedly-appointed-by-the-same-party--a-case-for-disqualification-.aspx.

83   **55 percent of all ISDS claims:** "Profiting from Injustice," by Pia Eberhardt and Cecilia Olivet, *Transnational Institute and Corporate Europe Observatory Report*, November 2012.

83   **apply only to their signatory countries:** *The International Law on Foreign Investment: Third Edition*, by Muthucumaraswamy Sornarajah, Cambridge University Press, 2010.

84   **"complementary and mutually reinforcing laws":** "The Emerging Global Regime for Investment" by Jeswald W. Salacuse, *Harvard International Law Journal*, 2010.

86   **CMS, Enron, Sempra, and LG&E:** *CMS Gas Transmission Company v. Argentina*, ICSID, award May 12, 2005, http://www.italaw.com/cases/288; *Enron Corporation Ponderosa Assets, L.P. vs. Argentina*, ICSID, award May 22, 2007, http://www.italaw.com/cases/401; *LG&E Energy Corp., LG&E Capital Corp., and LG&E International, Inc. v. Argentina*, ICSID, award July 25, 2007, http://www.italaw.com/cases/documents/624; *Sempra Energy International v. Argentina*, ICSID, award Sept. 28, 2007, http://www.italaw.com/cases/documents/1004.

87   **uniformly bad news:** "Necessity may not be invoked by a State as a ground for precluding the wrongfulness of an act not in conformity with an international obligation of that State unless the act: (a) Is the only way for the State to safeguard an essential interest against a grave and imminent peril; and (b) Does not seriously impair an essential interest of the State or States towards which the obligation exists, or of the international community as a whole.""Draft Articles on the Responsibility of States for Internationally Wrongful Acts with Commentaries," Article 25, U.N., 2001. http://untreaty.un.org/ilc/texts/instruments/english/commentaries/9_6_2001.pdf.

90   **a handful of men:** The same four arbitrators had served on almost every single one of the gas companies' tribunals. Francisco Orrego-Vicuña, the former ambassador to Chile, had served as president of CMS, Enron, and Sempra. Marc Lalonde, a Canadian ad hoc judge at the International Court of Justice, had served with Orrego Vicuña on CMS and Sempra. The remaining member of the CMS tribunal was Francisco Rezek, a Brazilian member of the International Court of Justice, who also sat on the LG&E tribunal

138

with Albert Jan van den Berg, a Dutchman, who served with Orrego Vicuña and Lalonde on Sempra.

91   three-person annulment committee: "ICSID Convention," Article 52. https://icsid.worldbank. org/ICSID/StaticFiles/basicdoc/ partA-chap04.htm.

92   unclear if that's how it actually works: *The Effect of Treaties on Foreign Direct Investment* by Karl P. Sauvant and Lisa E Sachs, Oxford University Press, ISDS may affect very particular kinds of investments in very particular cases, but it's difficult to identify broad statistical effects. See also "Bilateral Investment Treaties, Credible Commitment, and the Rules of (International) Law: Do BITs Promote Foreign Direct Investment?," by Jason Webb Yackee, *Law & Society Review*, Vol. 42, Issue 4, December 2008, pp. 805–832. Others argue that signing ISDS expressed a "culture of commitment," and was "part and parcel of effective good governance." See "The Market Economy and the State: Hayekian and Ordoliberal conceptions," by Manfred Streit and Michael Wohlgemuth, *The Theory of Capitalism in the German Economic Tradition*, Max Planck Institute of Economics, 2000. One study found a positive dynamic relationship between a country's commitment to investment treaties, and the

strengthening of the rule of law and democracy. "The Effect of BITs on Regulatory Quality and the Rule of Law in Developing Countries" by Cesar Aranguri. http://www.iilj. org/research/documents/if2010-11.aranguri.1.pdf.

92   "Today's policy literature is filled with extravagant claims": "Foreign Direct Investment, Productivity, and Country Growth: An Overview," by Silvio Contessi and Ariel Weinberger, *Federal Reserve Bank of St. Louis Review*, March/April 2009, Vol. 91, issue 2, pp. 61–78.

92   "Investors rarely, if ever, enter a foreign market because of ISDS protections": "Transatlantic trade and investment negotiations: Reaching a consensus on investor-state dispute settlement," by Miriam Sapiro, Brookings Institution, Global Views No. 5, October 2015. http:// www.brookings.edu/~/media/ Research/Files/Papers/2015/10/ transatlantic-trade-investment-negotiations-sapiro/ GlobalViews5Oct2015_FINAL.pdf.

93   refused to sign any BITs that include ISDS provisions: Brazil signed 14 BITs during the 1990s, but so far has refused to ratify any of them. "Delayed Ratification: The Domestic Fate of Bilateral Investment Treaties," by Yoram Z. Haftel and Alexander Thompson, *International Organization*, Vol.

67, Issue 02, April 2013, pp. 355–387. As it has become more of a capital exporting nation in recent years, Brazil has ratified some investment treaties that do not include ISDS provisions. "Brazil's New Investment Treaties: Outside Looking... Out?," by Pedro Martini, Kluwer Arbitration Blog, June 16, 2015. http://kluwerarbitrationblog.com/2015/06/16/brazils-new-investment-treaties-outside-looking-out-2/.

93 **"I don't see how that's good for the domestic courts":** See also, "Eyes wide shut on ISDS," by Lisa Sachs and Lise Johnson, *The Hill*, April 22, 2015.

93 **pay $17.3 million to the companies:** *Mobil Investments Canada Inc. and Murphy Oil Corporation v. Canada*, ICSID under NAFTA, award February 20, 2015. http://www.italaw.com/cases/1225.

94 **threatened to withdraw:** "Bill to withdraw from the ICSID," Argentine National Congress, March 21, 2012. http://www1.hcdn.gov.ar/proyxml/expediente.asp?fundamentos=si&numexp-1311-D-2012.

95 **terminate their international investment treaties:** "The Uncertain Future of ICSID in Latin America," by Ignacio Vincentelli, Social Science Research Network, February 20, 2009. http://

papers.ssrn.com/sol3/papers.cfm?abstract_id=1348016.

95 **"harm done to the public welfare":** "Public Statement on the International Investment Regime," August, 31 2010. http://www.osgoode.yorku.ca/public-statement-international-investment-regime-31-august-2010/.

95 **European nations' sovereignty:** "EU Tries To Put Lipstick On The Corporate Sovereignty Pig," by Glyn Moody, Tech Dirt, May 7, 2015. https://www.techdirt.com/articles/20150506/10054030901/eu-tries-to-put-lipstick-corporate-sovereignty-pig.shtml.

97 **$75 million in compensation:** *Occidental Exploration and Production Co. v. Ecuador*, London Court of International Arbitration, July 1, 2004. http://ita.law.uvic.ca/documents/Oxy-EcuadorFinalAward_001.pdf.

98 **twice the country's GDP:** Chevron Annual Report, 2004. http://www.chevron.com/documents/pdf/unocal2004annualreport.pdf Occidental v. Ecuador, at para. 683.

98 **below the poverty line:** World Bank data. http://data.worldbank.org/indicator/SI.POV.NAHC/countries/EC?page=2&display=default.

139

140   101   **housing assistance:**
"Federal Housing Assistance
for Low-Income Households,"
Congressional Budget Office, Sept.
9, 2015. https://www.cbo.gov/
publication/50782.

101   **"To give you an idea":** "ICSID
orders Ecuador to pay $1.7 billion
to Occidental Petroleum," by Aldo
Orellana López, Network for Justice
in Global Investment, October
2012. http://justinvestment.
org/2012/10/icsid-orders-ecuador-
to-pay-1-7-billion-to-occidental-
petroleum-interview-with-the-
ecuador-decide-network/.

101   **express my dissent:**
*Occidental Petroleum Corporation
and Occidental Exploration and
Production Company v. The Republic
of Ecuador,* ICSID, award October
5, 2012. http://www.italaw.com/
cases/767.

102   **declaring ISDS inconsistent:**
"Denunciation of the ICSID
Convention and BITs: Impact on
Investor-State Claims," UNCTAD,
IIA Issues Note, December 2,
2010, http://unctad.org/en/Docs/
webdiaeia20106_en.pdf.

102   **Chevron's claim:** *Chevron
Corporation and Texaco Petroleum
Corporation v. Ecuador,* UNCITRAL.
http://www.italaw.com/cases/257.

102   ***The New Yorker:*** "Reversal of
Fortune," by Patrick Radden Keefe,
The New Yorker, January 9, 2012.

103   **award-winning
documentary:** *Crude,* directed by
Joe Berlinger. http://chevrontoxico.
com/crude/.

104   **"The game is up":**
"International Arbitration
Tribunal Finds Chevron Not
Liable For Environmental Claims
in Ecuador," Chevron Corporation
press release, September 2013.
https://www.chevron.com/stories/
international-arbitration-tribunal-
finds-chevron-not-liable-for-
environmental-claims-in-ecuador.

107   **a Canadian funeral
conglomerate:** Loewen Group, Inc.
and Raymond L. Loewen v. United
States, Award June 26, 2003. www.
italaw.com/cases/documents/634.

109   **"If we don't write the
new rules":** Remarks by the
President on Trade, May 8, 2015.
https://www.whitehouse.gov/
the-press-office/2015/05/08/
remarks-president-trade.

109   **"too small for the big
things":** *The End of the Free Market:
Who Wins the War Between States
and Corporations,* by Ian Bremmer,
Portfolio, 2010.

113   **liberals scowled:** And they
continue to. In 2015, for example,
the American left decried the
WTO's decision that a U.S.
consumer rights law requiring
meat-packers to label their
products indicating where an

animal had been born, raised, and slaughtered violated the WTO because it discriminated against imported meats. U.S. lawmakers ended up making the regulation voluntary in order to avoid sanctions. See also, "WTO rules against U.S. dolphin-safe canned tuna labels" by Krista Hughes, Reuters, April 14, 2015.

114 **contradictions of their own:** *The Regulation of International Trade*, 4th edition, by Michael Trebilcock, Robert Howse, and Antonia Eliason, Routledge, 2012. "Today, the protesters who march against globalization are not marching in favor of the state. Instead, they are mostly advocating a set of values and causes that transcend state boundaries and that require global action. Instead of advocating for a simple 'return' to the state, they are demanding that both domestic and global governance be subject to *international* norms external to the trading system, such as those of international human rights or biodiversity, and that both domestic and global governance be judged against conceptions of global justice, which themselves usually entail very significant restrictions on state sovereignty."

115 **Bilcon:** "Clayton/Bilcon vs. Government of Canada," $101 million in damages claimed. http://www.international.gc.ca/trade-agreements-accords-commerciaux/

topics-domaines/disp-diff/clayton.   141
aspx?lang=eng.

115 **an ideal set of rules:** U.S. officials point out that they've updated and improved the model U.S. bilateral investment treaty multiple times since the 1980s. While some older BITs still allow claims to be filed and heard in secret, most are now much more transparent. All ISDS tribunals conducted using both ICSID and UNCITRAL rules must now, as of 2014, be made mostly public. In 2015, the United Nations Convention on Transparency in Treaty-based Investor-State Arbitration was opened for signatures. See, for an example of incremental improvement, "US Releases Final Draft of Model BIT," by Luke Eric Peterson, Invest-SD News Bulletin, Dec. 17, 2004. http://www.iisd.org/pdf/2004/investment_investsd_dec17_2004.pdf.

115 **The investment chapter of the TPP:** Trans Pacific Partnership, Chapter 9: Investment, Final Text, 2015. https://ustr.gov/sites/default/files/TPP-Final-Text-Investment.pdf.

116 **robust and far-reaching:** For example: Annex 10-D, US-Chile FTA. The TPP reads: "except in rare circumstances, nondiscriminatory regulatory actions by a Party that are designed and applied to protect legitimate public welfare objectives,

142   such as public health, safety, and the environment, do not constitute indirect expropriations."

116   **nothing to worry about:** "Investor-State Dispute Settlement (ISDS) Questions and Answers," by Jeffrey Zients, White House Blog, February 26, 2015. https://www.whitehouse.gov/blog/2015/02/26/investor-state-dispute-settlement-isds-questions-and-answers.

116   **Investment Court System:** "Transatlantic Trade and Investment Partnership: Trade in Services, Investment, and E-Commerce, Chapter 11," European Union's proposal for Investment Protection and Resolution of Investment Disputes, tabled for discussion on November 12, 2015. http://trade.ec.europa.eu/doclib/docs/2015/november/tradoc_153955.pdf.

117   **a court-like structure:** "Enhancing International Investment Law's Legitimacy: Conceptual and Methodological Foundations of a New Public Law Approach" by Stephan W. Schill, *Virginia Journal of International Law*, 2001. http://www.vjil.org/assets/pdfs /vol52/issue1/Schill_Final.pdf. "An International Investment Regime?," by Konrad von Moltke, the International Institute for Sustainable Development, 2000. http://e15initiative.org/publications/the-international-investment-law-and-policy-regime-challenges-and-options/.

117   **exhaust domestic judicial channels:** "ISDS in the EU's International Investment Agreements, Volume 1, Workshop," letter to the European Parliament from Steffen Hindelang. "[I]nternational investment law and investor-state dispute settlement can only regain legitimacy if the latter does not aim at replacing or turning into an alternative to domestic administrative and judicial safeguards, but instead backs them up in case of failure." http://www.europarl.europa.eu/RegData/etudes/STUD/2014/534979/EXPO_STU(2014)534979_EN.pdf.

117   **"Zombie ISDS":** "The Zombie ISDS: Rebranded as ICS, rights for corporations to sue states refuse to die," Corporate Europe, February 17, 2016. http://corporateeurope.org/sites/default/files/attachments/the_zombie_isds_0.pdf.

119   **governments stand to gain from the system:** "Withdrawing from Investment Treaties but Protecting Investment," by Clint Peinhardt and Rachel L. Wellhausen, under review, April 2016. http://www.rwellhausen.com/uploads/6/9/0/0/6900193/peinhardt_wellhausen_bitwithdrawal.pdf.

Columbia Global Reports is a publishing imprint from Columbia University that commissions authors to do original on-site reporting around the globe on a wide range of issues. The resulting novella-length books offer new ways to look at and understand the world that can be read in a few hours. Most readers are curious and busy. Our books are for them.

globalreports.columbia.edu